Strange Liverpool

Published by The Bluecoat Press, Liverpool
Book design by MARCH Graphic Design Studio, Liverpool
Printed by Ashford Colour Press

ISBN 1 904438 31 8

Tom Slemen

STRANGE LIVERPOOL

The Bluecoat Press

Contents

Introduction

In the course of my researches for the Haunted Liverpool series of books, I am usually to be found sitting at a machine for several hours at a time in the Central Library in William Brown Street, painstakingly viewing microfilmed copies of newspapers from the nineteenth and twentieth centuries, searching for unusual stories from Liverpool's past until my eyes hurt and my head aches. The omniscient Internet is also a valuable tool for historical research, but I still prefer the hands-on experience of trawling through old documents at the Liverpool Record Office, or blissfully thumbing through dusty, out-of-print books at places such as Quiggins, local charity shops, or amongst the dusty shelves of antiquarian booksellers. Reid of Liverpool, on Mount Pleasant, is a particularly well-stocked second-hand bookshop with many invaluable old tomes relating to the local history of my home town on its shelves.

The staff at the Liverpool Record Office at the Central Library have also invariably been extremely helpful, especially Kevin Roach, who has assisted me in unearthing many a fascinating local mystery through his diligent research into the vast archives stored at the library.

Whilst carrying out research for the Haunted Liverpool volumes, I often come across accounts that are strange and unusual but not always wholly supernatural in nature. I could not ignore such a rich seam of local stories and have therefore collected these articles in a box file labelled 'Strange Liverpool' and it has been to these that I have turned to produce this book.

You will still find a smattering of ghosts, leprechauns, vampires and premonitions in this book, because sometimes the world of the strange overlaps into the sphere of the supernatural. It cannot be avoided; but you will also read, amongst other tales, about the King of Everton, the scandal of Sandbag Daly's bogus funerals, the tragic end of Mickey the chimpanzee, the Secret Mersey Tunnel, the Liverpool Earthquake, the riddle of Old Swan's mass grave, and so on. Do I have a particular favourite? Well, I have a real fondness for the charming, bittersweet tale of Johnny McGuire's Gang – a group of little Victorian housebreakers reminiscent of Fagin and Oliver Twist.

When I was a child I would often visit my grandmother Rose Slemen and would love to listen, spellbound, as she told me magical tales of Liverpool's past. She would tell me about characters such as Spring-Heeled Jack, the Galosher Man, Madge Kirby, the Teacher Clock, and the McGuire Gang. The stories were seemingly endless and my young imagination was fired by my Gran's tales of the Angels of Mons, of Dashing Dan – a modern-day, self-styled knight, and of an enigmatic woman known as Silent Jane, who never spoke to anyone, although she still had the ability to talk.

My Gran was certainly the person who inspired me to record these fascinating stories and research others, and so ensure that they are not lost to future generations. By reading the stories in this book, I hope that you will experience some of the intrigue and wonder I felt when I first listened to them as a child.

Tom Slemen
2005

The McGuire Gang

A Liverpool street gang

Nine-year-old Johnny McGuire and his gang of juvenile housebreakers struggled to survive in the spiritual and moral darkness of Victorian Liverpool, a situation that thankfully exists no more. All that is known about Johnny's methods is that he had somehow obtained a blowlamp, probably through an act of thievery, in July 1886, and that he proceeded to use it skilfully to melt locks and padlocks in order to gain access to any premises which might contain something of value.

Johnny and his four friends, Tommy McKee and Bob Betley, both aged eight, Jimmy Moth, aged nine, and little Maggie Cowan – all of seven years old – were all orphans. They would have been totally destitute had it not been for the shelter and food that they were given by a shadowy, but apparently benevolent, character named Nel Shacklady. Shacklady lived on an old barge which was almost permanently moored on a secluded stretch of the Leeds and Liverpool Canal near Vauxhall Road. Shacklady was an eighty-one-year-old Romany woman, and her seven sons were all tinkers.

McGuire's gang were always seen to go to ground between Old Hall and Tithebarn Streets, and three policemen who had beats interlacing those thoroughfares became obsessed with catching the diminutive burglars. But Police Constables Read, Creighton and Carey were always just one step behind the gang, and were often thwarted, at the last moment, by the wiliness and agility of their quarry. Like lightning, the street urchins would make their escape in any way they could. They could climb fences and walls like monkeys, and on one hair-raising occasion the gang vanished through an impossibly narrow gap in a fence, with thickset PC Creighton in close pursuit. Purple with rage and frustration, the stout copper cursed the bratlings, and became well and truly stuck in the fence in his over-enthusiastic attempts to collar them.

One grim November evening, in 1886, Johnny McGuire and his team were lurking, as usual, in the dingy alleyways off Scotland Road, casing shops with a view to breaking into them, when they happened to see a bunch of arsonists running at full pelt from the rear of King and Heywood's drapery store. Flames were already visible flickering at the windows of the building. With no wish to be held responsible for the blaze, the gang fled, but were soon spotted by a policeman, who chased them as far as Bevington Bush Road, at which point the children seemed to vanish into thin air in the ill-lit warren of alleyways and courts. However, the gang was finally cornered in a cul-de-sac off Old Hall Street by Constables Read, Creighton and Carey.

The small door that led to the coal yards, and which also gave access to Shacklady's barge, had been padlocked by Creighton earlier in the evening. When Johnny came across the padlock he immediately thought about turning the blowlamp on it but soon realised that there wasn't enough time even to light it, let alone use it on the lock. They all knew that they were in a very tight corner and little Maggie Cowan began to sob and hid behind the boys.

"You're all going to get the cat-o'-nine tails!" PC Creighton cackled, as he and his two colleagues closed in on their quarry at last. McGuire and his little cronies had evaded them for long enough and made them look like fools in front of their colleagues, now it was time to extract their revenge.

"You don't want tiddlers, lads," came a rough voice suddenly from behind the three policemen. "Try catching the big fish."

A row of seven motley, tough-looking ruffians stood threateningly a few yards behind them them, blocking off their exit from the cul-de-sac. The men were armed with a menacing array of knives, chains and coshes and the three policemen instantly recognised them as members of the infamous Logwood Gang – the sworn enemies of the even more notorious High Rip Gang.

McGuire and his friends lost no time in grasping the opportunity to make their escape, as the Logwood Gang proceeded to give the cornered policemen a severe beating. Then, at a signal from their leader, the gang eventually stopped their assault and smirked with satisfaction as the gang leader gave the three trembling policemen another warning to, "Leave the little 'uns alone". By the time the policemen had staggered back to the station, nursing their bruises, the young gangsters were tucking into a hearty supper on Nel Shacklady's barge and she was laughing at their latest exploits.

Early on the cold grey morning of Good Friday, 8 April 1887, two of McGuire's gang, Jimmy Moth and Maggie Cowan, left the comparative comfort of Nel Shacklady's barge on the canal off Vauxhall Road and walked, barefoot, to the 'Holy Land' district of south Liverpool; a neighbourhood of which they had fond memories, as they had both lived there when their parents had been alive. In the miserable dawn light other ragged, barefoot children were sneaking about this neighbourhood, as the ancient local custom of 'Judas Burning' got underway. At Harlow Street the children rendezvoused with another youngster, Billy 'Puddin' O'Neil, a cousin of Maggie's. He was clutching a battered-looking effigy of Judas Iscariot in his arms and an inflated pig's bladder in his hand.

The three children rushed off to burn the Judas on the bonfire which they had prepared on a piece of waste land. Unfortunately, somewhere along the line, Maggie told Puddin' O'Neil all about a local 'job' which the gang had planned for Easter Sunday morning. The minute she had let the secret out of the bag she knew that she would be in trouble with Johnny; the gang had all been warned to keep their activities strictly secret. Puddin', in particular, should have been kept in the dark. He had always desperately wanted to be in McGuire's gang, but Johnny didn't trust him for some reason; probably because of his reputation for having a loose tongue and his obsession with food, both of which could get in the way when they were on a 'job'.

Around four o'clock on the following Sunday morning, McGuire's gang took advantage of a swirling raw fog that had crept up from the river and made their way under its cover to the narrow alleyway of Back Canning Place. A small folding ladder was placed against a backyard wall, and Johnny McGuire was the first to climb it. Having gained entry to the backyard, he silently lifted the latch of the gate and watched as his four partners in crime tiptoed into the yard. He was surprised, then angered, to see that Puddin' O'Neil had tagged along and was trying to sneak in behind the others without being noticed.

"Who told him about the job?" snapped Johnny with a frown, surveying his gang, and immediately everyone looked at Maggie, who had her guilty head bowed.

"You just can't keep that little mouth of yours shut, can you, Maggie?" he hissed, between gritted teeth. Then, turning to Puddin' he said, "Well, you're here now, I suppose, but don't you dare muck things up, or you'll be for it! Got it?"

A single panel in the back door was staved in and the little criminals gained entry to the house of wealthy merchant Horatio Robinson, a man who was rumoured to keep a large fortune stashed in a chest under the eaves of his house. The gang thoroughly and professionally searched the house as Robinson and his servants slept, but could not find the fabled chest in the garret, or anywhere else. They whispered to one another in the gypsy slang they had learned from Nel Shacklady and eventually Johnny instructed his accomplices and Puddin' to make their way quietly back down to the yard, as it looked as if this was a failed job.

The children tiptoed back down the carpeted stairs and meanwhile, dare-devil Johnny couldn't resist taking a peek into the master's bedroom. Not one to give up easily, he had decided to crawl under Robinson's bed, while he was asleep, in search of the money. It had to be there, they'd looked everywhere else.

As he was about to turn the doorknob of the bedroom, a youngish woman, dressed in black and with a ghastly pale face, emerged from one of the rooms further down the landing, and turned to face him. The candle which she was holding made the dark circles round her eyes stand out grotesquely and she gawked at him in shock and disbelief. Johnny's courage deserted him. His body went slack and he let go of the door handle. He was convinced that the woman was a ghost, appearing as she did at that hour in the morning and looking so pale and sinister.

The lady then spoke, "Alexander, my darling, you have returned to me at last!"

She threw out her arms and rushed along the landing towards McGuire, who let out a throttled scream, then bolted down the stairs two at a time. He could not have known that Lady Rose Hughes had recently suffered a nervous breakdown following the death of her beloved nine-year-old child Alexander, from peritonitis, and also that, bizarrely, the boy had been a replica of Johnny McGuire – an almost exact double.

The usual gang members had had a narrow escape that morning, but Puddin' O'Neil had tarried in the pantry looking for food, and was grabbed by one of the servants in the yard as he was tucking into a large meat pie from the larder. The master of the house, Mr Robinson, was about to summon the police, when his daughter, Lady Rose, stopped him. On the verge of hysteria, she told Puddin' that if he would take her to the boy she had seen on the landing, she would not press charges, but instead would give him a reward. The grief stricken Lady Rose longed to raise that boy as her own. In her confused mind she really did think that Johnny McGuire was some kind of miraculous reincarnation of her beloved Alexander and she longed to fill the aching hole he had left when he died. Robinson had no intention of allowing such a thing to happen, but in order to placate his daughter and at the same time find out where the little villains were hiding, he decided to go along with his daughter's wishes for the time being.

That morning the fog worsened, and a very nervous Puddin' O'Neil led a reluctant Robinson and his distraught weeping daughter through a succession of squalid, gloomy courts and Cimmerian back streets to Shacklady's barge by blazing torchlight. Neither Robinson nor Rose had ever been exposed to the abject poverty of Liverpool's darker side and they both felt decidedly ill at ease, expecting to be set upon by villains at every turn. As they approached the barge Robinson could restrain himself no longer and called to a policeman walking his beat for assistance. The gang was collared just as they were tucking into their breakfast on the canal barge.

Shacklady and her sons were forced to move on, as the police accused her of harbouring the young criminals, and they settled miles away to the north. Lady Rose's desire to adopt Johnny McGuire was thwarted by her father who dismissed the proposition as abject nonsense, solely inspired by her delicate mental state. However, it was said that the resourceful Johnny McGuire did quite well for himself, regardless. He emigrated to the United States when he was fifteen and apparently became quite a successful businessman in Texas.

Tommy McKee, Bob Betley, Jimmy Moth and Maggie Cowan were cared for at the Myrtle Street Orphanage for a while, and all were subsequently placed in well-to-do families. Maggie lived to a ripe old age and passed away in New Zealand at her grandson's farm in the 1970s. Although she ended her days living in relative luxury, she would often talk about her barefoot days in old Liverpool, and of her wild adventures as a member of Johnny McGuire's gang. Maggie had particularly fond memories of old Nel Shacklady, who had treated the children of the gang as if they were her own, feeding them and giving them shelter when the rest of the world had turned against them.

After the betrayal and arrest of Johnny McGuire and his gang upon that Easter Sunday morning, Billy Puddin' O'Neil was always referred to as Judas O'Neil.

Puddin' O'Neil

The Mystery of the Mass Grave

Old Swan mass grave

One of the greatest and most enduring mysteries in Liverpool's history started to unfold in the autumn of 1973, when a gang of workmen set about clearing a patch of land to build a two-storey Roman Catholic primary school between St Oswald Street and Montague Road, in Old Swan. The £450,000 St Oswald's Primary School would be built on scrubland close to the church, and Father Patrick James McCartney warned the workmen that they were likely to come across a few graves during their excavations, but no one at that point anticipated the sinister, macabre secret which would soon be revealed at the site.

Work commenced and, sure enough, an unmarked coffin was soon unearthed, quickly followed by another one, but the foreman, Thomas Breen, instructed his men to carry on excavating, and the coffins were solemnly placed to one side with the utmost respect. However, the workmen soon discovered that in an area some forty yards square, there were masses of coffins neatly piled sixteen high. Building work was immediately suspended, and the Clerk of Works came to take a look at the unusual find. It soon became obvious that they had uncovered a mass grave, and the total number of coffins discovered would eventually total an unbelievable 3,561. The mystery then deepened, because there were no records of any mass burial in the registers of St Oswald's Church. This seemed to indicate that the 3,561 bodies had been stacked in the ground at some time prior to 1840 – the year when the registration of burials became compulsory.

Local and national historians were naturally intrigued by the Old Swan mass grave, and some theorised that the dead must have been plague or cholera victims, but people who had died of such diseases were usually put in quicklime, without coffins. Furthermore, the dates of the plagues and cholera outbreaks in Liverpool and the numbers of the victims, as well as the time window within which they were buried, simply did not tally with the facts regarding the mass burial at Old Swan. Some historians even proposed that the answer to the baffling discovery might have something to do with the Benedictine Fathers who built a church in the vicinity of the site in the eighteenth century.

Before the historians had the chance to examine the mysterious coffins, the Home Office ordered Liverpool City Council to cordon off the mass grave with a ten-foot-high security fence. Officials in Whitehall subsequently gave instructions to cremate the unknown dead and to deposit their remains at Anfield Cemetery. The workmen had to wait a further eighteen months before the building of the school could recommence, and in the meantime, the media was warned off when a series of reporters attempted to discover exactly what had been found off St Oswald Street. The news leaked out that investigators had deduced that the 3,561 bodies had all been buried at the same time, which meant that it certainly hadn't been a plague pit, or a paupers' grave. What then, was the truth behind the mystery of the Old Swan mass grave?

In 1995, several historians contacted Whitehall, hoping to discover why the Home Office had given orders to cremate the unknown dead of Old Swan, and a spokesman said he couldn't trace any records of the incident. All the files relating to the mysterious mass grave had apparently been destroyed. The puzzle then, of how 3,561 bodies came to be buried off St Oswald Street, remained unsolved.

In times of plague and cholera epidemics the bodies of the victims were unceremoniously dumped in pits which were often filled with quicklime to try and halt the spread of infection. However, the thousands of bodies unearthed at Old Swan were not only placed in coffins, but they had been buried in groups according to their age, which suggests that all of the interments took place simultaneously. This means there are two possible explanations, both of which are controversial.

Could it be possible that over three thousand people were massacred at Old Swan at some time in the 1840s, or perhaps a decade before? If we suppose that there had been some kind of uprising, and that the authorities had dealt with the revolt by massacring the dissenters, would they afterwards have carefully buried the victims in coffins? Thousands of poor people were disembowelled and hanged by the authorities in England during the Peasants' Revolt of 1382, but even in those far off days, news of the massacre could not be contained, and soon spread across the entire country. Old Swan was a small, peaceful, rural suburb when the bodies were buried there en masse, therefore news of any rebellion and subsequent carnage would surely have been impossible to suppress.

The only clue that seems to provide a feasible solution to this mystery lies in several curious reports from council workmen who claimed that a few of the coffins did, in fact, bear name-plates. If these reports are true, then this could point to an intriguing possibility never considered before; that the coffins were moved from another graveyard and reburied at Old Swan. In 1838, the foundation stone to St George's Hall was laid. At that time, the site excavated for the hall's foundations lay adjacent to St John's Church. The grand building to be erected was extremely important, as not only would it contain a hall of unprecedented proportions, but it would also house the Assize Courts. However, for the work to proceed, many of the 82,491 coffins in St John's churchyard had to be removed to create space. The army of builders and civil engineers working on the St George's Hall project also suggested that the unsightly St John's Church itself should be demolished, as it would prove to be an eyesore out of all proportion to the proposed monumental building, worthy of ancient Greece. An infirmary and a lunatic asylum had already been levelled to make way for the hall, but now there was the thorny problem of the church graveyard to contend with, and herein lies the clue to the origin of the Old Swan Mass grave.

The orderly and precise way in which the coffins had been neatly stacked at Old Swan smacked of military involvement. All of the bodies with teeth intact – indicating that they were young when they died – were placed in one particular section of the burial site, and the coffins were perfectly aligned. Around the time frame in which the bodies were deposited at Old Swan –

around 1838 to 1840 – one major building project was underway in Liverpool: St George's Hall. It is thought that many thousands of the 82,491 graves were moved from St John's churchyard, which partially overlapped the building site. Who actually moved these graves, and where were they moved to?

Well, old maps of the area contain some of the clues. On one map of Liverpool in the early 1840s a huge army barracks can be seen standing next to the building site cleared for St George's Hall. It takes no stretch of the imagination to envisage the authorities secretly enlisting the help of the regiment stationed at these barracks to transport the coffins exhumed from St John's churchyard to a new burial site. The assignment would have been carried out in strictest secrecy because of the delicate nature of the exhumation and reburial.

In 1868, for example, two thousand coffins were removed from the graveyard of St Peter's Church on Church Street and re-interred at Anfield Cemetery. The coffins at Old Swan had been buried simultaneously, in perfect alignment, and this would have required considerable manpower and organisation to achieve. To an army of trained military men, equipped with spades, the task would have been perfectly possible and could have been completed within days. The early railway, which ran from Lime Street to the Liverpool suburbs, could have been used to secretly transport the coffins – under the cover of darkness – to the new burial site in the rural open spaces of early nineteenth century Old Swan.

This is all just theory and conjecture, of course, and the solution to the Old Swan mass grave conundrum may well lie in some other direction. Thomas Breen, the foreman who oversaw the removal of the bodies in the mass grave, is now in his seventies and lives in Woolton, and he vividly recalls that there were no infants among the dead, which does pose a problem to the theory about the bodies being transplanted from an existing churchyard. Surely there would have been the full age range amongst the dead? Mr Breen also remarked that the coffin wood proved almost impossible to burn and a lot of it had to be buried on the site of the new school. Perhaps if some of this wood could be recovered today, there may be some traces of DNA material to be had, however slight.

Mr Breen told me how, at one point during the gruesome excavation, the perfectly preserved body of a young woman with long reddish hair and dressed in a white garment, slid out of a damaged coffin and landed in the rain-soaked mud with a sickening thud. The grave-diggers then watched in horror as, within minutes, her pretty face and youthful body started to disintegrate, as the effects of the atmosphere set in. When the rain worsened at one point, one young grave-digger found himself sinking into an unwholesome quagmire, with numerous bodies slithering out of their decaying coffins into the malodorous mud. The excavation pit became totally waterlogged and the whole scene was reminiscent of a scene from the film Poltergeist, with coffins splitting open and spilling out skeletons and decayed corpses into the filthy water, making the workmen's jobs not just unpleasant but almost impossible.

The Home Office has suspiciously 'lost' the files referring to the Old Swan mass graves burial site, so it may be some time before we learn the full truth about this enduring mystery.

Old Swan mass grave

Sandbag Daly

In the last breaths of the dying day of 4 May 1941, a dangerous, first-quarter moon already hung over a Liverpool at war. Before the greatest conflict in the history of mankind, the moon had been an object of occasional mild curiosity and romance, but now its silvery radiance was transformed into an accursed spotlight which enabled the Nazi pilots to locate their night-time targets. The cratered city was blacked out, and the emergency services and traumatised civilians were desperately trying to cope with the calamitous aftermath of Hitler's Angels of Death – the long-range bombers, such as the Junkers JU 88, Focke-Wulf Fw 2000, and Heinkel He III.

"If you're going through Hell, keep going!" was Churchill's advice, and Liverpool had certainly been infernal of late. Just the day before, the *SS Malakand*, a steamer loaded with over one thousand tons of shells and bombs, was destroyed by enemy action in Huskisson No 2 dock. Four people lost their lives, and fragments of the ship were later found scattered up to two and a half miles away from the dock.

Upon this particular Sunday night, the Nazi bombers took off from occupied France, headed for the Bristol Channel, flew due north across Cardigan Bay, then east-north-east over Angelsey, towards their target – Liverpool. The history of the Liverpool Blitz is well documented, but here is just one tragic story from those dark days.

Isabella Gibson, aged fifty, and her teenaged son Clifford, were severely injured that Sunday when a bomb hit the air-raid shelter in which they had taken refuge at Back Castle Street in Walton. The mother and son died three days later. William Humphrey Smith, a thirty-eight-year-old auxiliary fireman of 13 Lydiate Street, Lodge Lane, was seriously injured on 2 May 1941 at Riversdale Road, Aigburth, and died from his injuries the next day at the David Lewis Northern Hospital. The families of these victims of the May Blitz called upon the services of Daly & Co Ltd, a respected firm of funeral directors with premises on Scotland Road.

The manager of the undertakers, fifty-year-old Michael Daly of Woodbine Street, Kirkdale, and his clerk and bookkeeper, thirty-three-year-old John

Murnaghan, of Knowsley Lane, Whiston, made all the arrangements for the funerals, and then set off to collect the bodies of Mrs Gibson and Mr Smith from the mortuaries at County Road and the Northern Hospital respectively, but the men were unable to find the bodies. Daly and Murnaghan were driven to the mortuaries by John Joseph Darke, a hearse driver. Darke then drove the undertakers to Byrom Hall mortuary, but still the cadavers of Smith and Gibson could not be located. In the widespread pandemonium of a city reeling from a week of unrelenting bombardment, there was naturally a great deal of confusion, and the morgues were filled well beyond capacity.

Darke then drove the funeral director and his clerk to Rose Hill Police Station, where Daly telephoned an attendant at a smaller mortuary, but the corpses of Smith and Gibson weren't there either. Daly and Murnaghan, frustrated at having no bodies to bury, resorted to filling two coffins with bags of sand and passing them off as the dearly departed. Daly told John Darke about the ruse, and explained that he had had to do it because the bodies of Smith and Gibson had obviously been buried in a communal grave and he did not want to disappoint the relatives.

"This places me in a really bad position," Darke complained, and threatened to abandon the hearse on the way to the funeral.

"For the relatives' sake the funerals must be carried out!" Daly ranted, and he eventually persuaded Darke to drive the hearse to the first cemetery in Anfield and then take the second coffin to a cemetery in Everton. The funeral services went ahead, and the sand-filled coffins were solemnly interred as the weeping mourners lined the gravesides, completely unaware of the scandalous deception which had been perpetrated.

Daly and Murnaghan would have got away with it but not long afterwards the heinous truth came to light when the bodies of Smith and Gibson were found, unclaimed, at mortuaries elsewhere in the city. One of the bogus graves was exhumed at Anfield Cemetery, and the findings sent detectives straight to Mr Daly's Kirkdale home.

Daly and Murnaghan were tried at St George's Hall and charged with falsifying entries in the register of burials. John Joseph Darke, the hearse driver, was called as a witness and gave damning evidence against his boss and Murnaghan. He told the shocked court how he was coerced into taking part in the trickery against his better judgement. Daly and Murnaghan pleaded guilty, and were bound over for two years. 'Sandbag' Daly – as he became known – was also ordered to pay £20 court costs.

Silent Jane

Standing proudly at the junction of Paradise Street and Park Lane, the popular church of St Thomas once stood. The church – built in 1750 – was mostly attended by Liverpool's wealthy families and moneyed merchant princes. At this church, the famous local eccentric Joseph Williamson was married, and when he died in 1840, he was interred in St Thomas's graveyard. Williamson was known as The Mole, because of his mania for having tunnels excavated beneath the streets of Edge Hill, and his subterranean labyrinth is now open to the public.

Another figure of curiosity who prayed beneath the 216-foot spire of St Thomas' was one Jane Redfern, a beautiful, well-educated and refined young woman known locally as 'Silent Jane' because she spoke to no one, not even the reverend of St Thomas's where she attended Mass regularly. That she had the ability to speak was not in question, because she sang the hymns wonderfully during the church services.

One Sunday morning at 11pm, in the summer of 1872, over a thousand people were crammed into the church to hear Mass, when the service was disrupted by the hysterical sobbing of a young woman named Lucy Robinson, of Falkner Street. She rushed down the aisle and scanned the rows of shocked and outraged faces until she spotted the angelic visage of Jane Redfern who sat impassively in one of the pews. Miss Robinson screamed at Jane and accused her of bewitching her fiancé. Silent Jane ignored her and stared straight ahead at the altar. She made no reply, as usual. Most of the congregation were aware that many of the men in the parish, both young and old, were captivated by the beautiful Jane Redfern, but the mute object of their affection never showed them any interest in return.

The curate, the Reverend Samuel Ireson, glared down from the pulpit at Miss Robinson and ordered her to leave the church at once. The distressed woman was duly escorted from the church by a friend.

Ironically, the Reverend Ireson, who lived two doors away from Lucy Robinson, at 50 Falkner Street, had himself made passes at Silent Jane, and the organist at the church, John Fritton, had also fallen under Redfern's spell and had almost come to blows with the Reverend Ireson and other rivals who sought the attention of the mysterious beauty. Of course, Silent Jane was hated by many of the ladies of nineteenth century Liverpool polite society, as they were well aware of the reaction she provoked in their menfolk. And why did she never speak? Was she harbouring some scandalous secret? Or was she just plain rude?

After Jane Redfern had attended evening Mass at St Thomas's on Thursdays, she would walk the short distance back to her Toxteth home and often find herself being followed by a train of love-sick admirers ranging from Rodney Street physicians to the most humble parishioner. Their love was always unrequited – the only kind of love that lasts forever.

From my own research into this enigmatic lady, I can reveal that when she was eighteen she had fallen madly in love with a man from Cumbria who was extremely jealous and possessive. He watched young Jane like a hawk and constantly told her that she must speak to no man other than himself. Despite this, people who knew the young couple said they were made for one another, and they planned to marry and then move to the Lake District. However, this was not to be. Tragedy struck when the man Jane worshipped contracted some kind of fever and died. On his deathbed he made her promise that she would not forsake him, even after he was dead, and Jane vowed she would never speak to another man until she joined him in Heaven.

She was true to her word and not only never looked for love again on this earth, but also never spoke to another man for the rest of her life. She died in obscurity in Edwardian times.

The Summer of the Leprechaun

All of the old legends and folklore from every part of this planet seem to tell of a secret commonwealth of mystical beings who live invisibly alongside us. These beings, variously referred to as elves, devils, leprechauns, lutins, the Feadh-Ree, fairies, boggarts, trolls and other legendary names, are said to be grouped into various species, and for most of the time, we are as unaware of them as we are of the grotesque monsters of the microscopic world who inhabit our mattresses and soft furnishings munching away on flakes of our dead skin. Dust mites would appear to us as terrifying alien creatures if they were on a similar scale to ourselves, but until the invention of optical and electron microscopes we were totally unaware of their existence.

Could there be creatures around you as you read these words that are presently unknown to modern science? Our eyes perceive only a small, narrow slit of the total electromagnetic spectrum which contains all of the radiations of the universe. Red, orange, yellow, green, blue, indigo and violet, and all of the shades in between those colours, are all that we can perceive with our eyes. We are blind to infra-red, ultraviolet and countless other invisible 'colours'. To be able to see the craters of the Moon we had to invent the telescope to enhance and enlarge the image for our feeble eyes, and to see our own blood corpuscles we had to devise the microscope, because our eyes have fixed lenses like a cheap throwaway camera.

Our ears also have their limitations, depending on our age. Human hearing differs vastly from the acute hearing abilities of dog and cats and many wild animals, and a human being's limited listening range is determined not only by age, but by hereditary factors as well. Our sense of smell, once highly important to man for survival in prehistoric times, is now swamped by chemicals from deodorants, aftershaves, perfumes, air-fresheners and so on. Our senses of vision and hearing are restricted, and our sense of smell has been made almost redundant, and even our most basic survival instincts are being progressively eliminated by the society mankind has created. We are protected from danger and violence by armies and the police, whereas in ancient times we had to look after ourselves, and all we had were primitive weapons and our human instincts. We could smell animals such as sabre-toothed tigers and bears lying in wait for us, or spot them lying low in the undergrowth, or the shadows of a cave, but now our senses in the modern world are so dulled that we can step off a pavement into the path of a bright red double-decker bus that we didn't notice.

It's the same with our food and drink, which is analysed, processed, irradiated, filtered and treated with antibiotics and all kinds of artificial additives before being elaborately packaged. Again, we are cocooned from the reality our ancestors lived in and modern children often have little idea of where food comes from. The ancients were fitter than us, and ate wholesome, undoctored food. Their water was not filtered or tampered with; their wines contained no chemicals such as copper sulphate – just the produce of the grape. In many ways their minds were sharper than ours, as can be seen by the staggering feats of engineering such as Stonehenge and the pyramids.

The ancients claimed to have a Third Eye, located traditionally in the brain just behind the centre of the forehead. This 'eye' perceived mystical impressions far too subtle for our coarser senses to register, and was regarded as the seat of intuition and heightened instincts. If we compare this to our patterns of consciousness today, we will admit to being in a state of trance most of the time, gawping mindlessly at television, or a computer monitor, as we surf the Internet. It is as if our hi-tech, sanitised world, compounded by television, film and computers, has turned us all into zombies who are entangled in self-woven nets of daydreams.

Across the world, attention spans are shrinking, drug and alcohol abuse is on the rise, and mindless television channels and idiotic violent video games are proliferating to feed robotic, stupefied minds. As a race, we have never been as out of touch with reality in our history. Long ago, when we worked in harmony with nature, living off the land, sowing and reaping by the seasons, and using our instincts to stay alive, we inhabited a whole different reality from our existence today. In those times there was an unquestioning belief in the existence of a supernatural race of beings. There was a symbiotic, balanced relationship between us and them. Their lands were never to be touched by human hands, or developed in any way, and their 'fairy paths' were to be kept clear from obstructions of any kind. Occasionally, mischievous members of the fairy race purloined or borrowed items from humans and sometimes even stole livestock, but on the whole, they kept to themselves.

They sometimes imparted remedies and miracle cures to humans and even melodious songs and catchy tunes, but the fairies mostly kept well away from man, woman and child. They gradually became very wary of mortals because of humanity's propensity for greed and aggression. The ancient fairies were regarded by man with some suspicion, as no one could be sure of their origins. Some maintained that the little people were fallen angels, or perhaps something God had created in the past which was never mentioned in the Bible. There was even once a theory that fairies were members of a small aboriginal race of Eskimos who had strayed into the northern extremities of Scotland! However, most of the legends across Western Europe stated that the fairies had been driven underground into caves and mounds by warrior bands of invading Celts.

In Britain and Ireland they mostly inhabited the western parts of the isles, with colonies in the outer isles of Scotland, the Isle of Man, Cornwall, Wales, Cheshire, Lancashire and Cumbria. Later invaders of our islands almost spelt extinction for the fairies, and when Christianity reached these shores, over-zealous friars and exorcists of the church swept across the land, blessing barns, fields, woods, streams and the remotest farmhouses. The new religion, brought here by St Augustine, the first Archbishop of Canterbury, in 597 AD, led to the establishment of a monastery at Kent, and although King Aethelbert cautiously welcomed the missionaries, he allowed them to preach and was even baptised by them himself in the end.

The 'old religion' however, did not die easily. At night, before roaring log fires, the old storytellers related enchanted tales of witches, ghosts, elves, fairies and trolls. The children would listen in wonder to the colourful stories of supernatural beings that no one was allowed to talk about anymore, because the new church had forbidden people to discuss anything paranormal. And yet, from Douglas to Liverpool, from County Clare to Derbyshire, from Angelsey to Alderley Edge, from Cornwall to Clitheroe, fireside tales of the fairy folk remained very popular late at night.

In the twentieth century – a long period of rational scepticism – the little people made an unlikely come-back at a time when a new mystery was capturing the imagination of the human race: the flying saucer phenomenon. In the summer of 1964, there was a wave of UFO sightings across the UK and parts of Western Europe, and there were many reports of classic flying saucer-type craft seen in the airspace over the North West of England. There has long been an undeserved association with flying saucers and little green men, so when alleged encounters with elf-like beings were reported in Britain that summer, in places such as the Isle of Man, Lancashire, North Wales, Cheshire and Cumbria, some Ufologists connected the reports of 'leprechauns' with the saucers, and hypothesised that the little people visiting from another planet were being mistaken for the fairies of old.

Locally, on 1 July 1964, a leprechaun mania broke out across Liverpool when a group of schoolchildren told bemused parents and teachers that they had seen little, green-skinned people wearing white hats in Jubilee Park, Jubilee Drive, in Kensington. The children's tales were naturally dismissed as immature imaginings – until adults also reported seeing strange things around Jubilee Drive. The first of these took place in the back garden of a Mrs Williams at her house on Edge Lane on the Wednesday afternoon of 1 July 1964. Pensioner Mrs Williams and her sixty-seven-year-old neighbour Mrs Jones, sat at a tea table they'd prepared in the sunny, secluded garden. Mrs Williams brought the hissing kettle from the kitchen and poured boiling water into the teapot on the table. Muffins and biscuits were laid on as usual, and the honey in the honey-pot had been collected from Mrs Jones's own bees.

It was a typical English afternoon tea on a glorious sunny afternoon, but when the women started to talk at the table, they found their conversation increasingly drowned out by the unusually loud chattering of magpies in the shrubberies at the bottom of the garden. Then Mrs Williams recoiled in shock, because something surreal and a little frightening stepped out from the stark shadows and into the bright sunlight. A figure, about two feet in height, or even less, with pale, yellow-green skin, stood there. He wore a small white helmet, very similar to the safety headgear worn by modern cyclists, and was clad in a one-piece suit which had the reflective texture of modern plastic. The face looked human, but rather childish, and it was much smaller than a normal face. The diminutive visitor also looked male, but he didn't stay there long, so they couldn't say for sure. Mrs Williams saw him too, but let out a squeal of surprise, and at this, the little being turned and fled into the shrubbery.

The women were too scared to go and investigate how the entity had gained entry into the garden, and the next morning Mrs Jones brought her nephew and his Alsatian dog to the bottom of Mrs William's garden – and there was a small opening in the fence where a rotten strip of wood had been broken. The nephew repaired the fence. He and his aunt noticed that the German shepherd dog was very uneasy while it was in the garden, and seemed to be able to see something which they couldn't.

That day, Mrs Jones was reading the Liverpool Echo, when she received quite a surprise. On page five of the newspaper, a small column, entitled, 'Leprechauns Go Bowling In The Park' stated:

> Thousands of children joined in a big hunt in Liverpool last night for – leprechauns. They invaded Jubilee Park in Jubilee Drive, hunted among the shrubberies, tore up some small plants and turf, scaled surrounding walls, and searched empty houses. The Great Leprechaun Hunt all started after someone had reported seeing little green men in white hats throwing stones and tiny clods of earth at one another on the bowling green the previous night. That story buzzed through all the schools in the area, and when the schools closed yesterday afternoon, the youngsters swarmed to the park. It was all too much for Irish parks constable James Nolan. "I don't believe in leprechauns myself," he said. He called in the city police. Police in cars and on motorcycles arrived. They cleared the hundreds of youngsters from the bowling greens – the reported playground of the wee folk – closed the gate, and stood guard.
>
> But beyond the bowling green gates the youngsters milled, tiny tots to fourteen-year-olds. They crammed the top of the covered reservoir for a better view of the bowling green. Tolerant bobbies wandered about trying to get the youngsters on the move. But the kids would not believe that there were no little green men. It was not until after 10pm that the park was cleared. How the story started was not known, but last night was the second night running of the leprechaun hunt. And how did those little brownies who help the Irish housewife with her chores come to arrive in Liverpool? Maybe they flew from old Ireland. A woman resident in Crosby last night reported seeing, "Strange objects glistening in the sky, whizzing over the river to the city from the Irish Sea."

Mrs Jones took the newspaper along to her neighbour, and Mrs Williams was thunderstruck by the peculiar report. Mrs Jones was a religious woman, and regarded the reports of the leprechauns as something sinister. A friend of hers who attended the local church of St Cyprian claimed that a vicar had warned her about the things "masquerading as fairies" for they were really of the devil, and out to undermine Christianity. Mrs Williams was a little more progressive in her way of thinking and disagreed with the vicar's views. She didn't quite know what to think but believed that the leprechauns might have something to do with the recent spate of flying saucer sightings across the country.

As the leprechaun mania grew in intensity throughout Liverpool, legions of expectant children stormed the city's parks. The little people were spotted in Abercromby Park, Stanley Park, Newsham Park and Sefton Park, where one thirteen-year-old girl said she even managed to grab hold of one little man but he slithered from her grasp and fled away laughing.

Around this time over two hundred children also invaded the sanctum of St Chad's Church in Kirkby to report to the Canon, John Lawton, of the little people they had seen locally. In one field near Kirkby, the elfin figures were seen dancing in the moonlight one night, and on the following day a type of corn circle was found at the scene. Weeks after that incident there were sightings of 'trolls' outside St Mary's Church in Northwood.

Alas, when that exciting summer of the leprechaun ended, the little visitors from elsewhere made themselves scarce – but will they return one day?

The Great Earthquake of 1931

At 1.25am, on 7 June 1931, bay windows inexplicably rattled and shattered in Anfield. At that same moment, a car being driven along Brook Street in Chester was swung around by a tremendous unseen force, and ploughed into a lamp-post. Meanwhile, on the other side of the Mersey, at Fairfield Crescent, Newsham, people in houses which rocked and shook were thrown out of their beds, and seconds after that nasty nocturnal surprise, Dr William Cookson of Great George's Road, Waterloo, was, in his own words, "Tossed high into the air from my bed like a pancake from a frying pan."

The Great North West England Earthquake of 1931 was deeply shocking to a population unused to such traumatic events. Earthquakes happened in exotic, far away places, not in England. People were as unprepared then as we are today for such a subterranean-born calamity.

Just before 1.30 on that eventful morning, at Lawrence Road, Wavertree, a man living at a house which had a reputation for being haunted, got the shock of his life when he awoke to find his bed moving steadily along the floor. The house was shuddering violently and the windows rattled spookily in their frames. The man – previously a devout sceptic regarding ghosts – ducked under the sheets and fervently said his prayers. For seven terrifying minutes, commencing at 1.25am, it seemed as if some angry giant beneath the earth was stirring from its slumbers.

One strange aspect of the earthquake was the simultaneous stopping of hundreds of clocks and watches in Southport, believed to have been caused by the tremors and electrical discharges in the atmosphere caused by the piezoelectric effects of subterranean rock pressure. At Southport's Bispham Road, a Mrs Eastham let out a scream when the quake struck, thinking that noisy burglars were at large in her home. Her husband took an old Persian sword from underneath the bed and began swiping at the imaginary intruders in the darkness.

Over on the Isle of Man, at that same moment, there was a series of terrifying landslides on the cliffs above Douglas Head which blocked the tramlines. St Helens felt the full force of the quake, with alleyway walls collapsing and chimney stacks toppling. Most bizarre of all was a house in Claughton Street which started to sink into the ground. After it had sunk several feet, it suddenly disintegrated and all that was left of it was a large mound of rubble and powder. Fortunately, the building was not occupied at the time. The man who lived next door to the collapsed house later told a Liverpool Echo reporter: "When the room shook I thought my supper was disagreeing with me."

Residents of Warrington also had a rude awakening that morning, with one old man being treated for shock when huge soot clouds blasted out at him from the bedroom fireplace as his chimney caved in. The cats and dogs of Warrington had been making a cacophony of mewing and barking that morning in the minutes leading up to the violent tremors, as if their sharpened senses had pre-warned them of the impending disaster. Today, many seismologists are in no doubt that certain creatures have a built in early-warning sense in their brains, which causes their behaviour to become erratic just before an earthquake strikes. If we could isolate the signals by which these animals are being alerted we might be able to predict when an earthquake is about to happen. Perhaps an electronic device could be tuned to the impulses so that a type of four-minute warning alert could be sounded before the tremors strike. This would allow early evacuation of buildings and would dramatically reduce the usual death toll from major earthquakes.

Minutes after the 1931 quake, the bells of the police switchboard at Hatton Garden jangled incessantly as the local populace panicked and demanded to know what was going on. An elderly colonel in Woolton rushed out of his house in his nightgown, firing an old elephant gun in the air as a warning shot to imagined invaders and would-be looters. As the mania gripped suburbia, two drunks on Shaw Street seized a policeman on his beat and claimed to have seen "a foreign army" alighting from a battleship at the Pier Head!

Seismologists reassured people living in dread of further tremors that the quake was a one-off event. Then, just over a week later, on 17 June, cars screeched to a halt and trams were brought to a standstill on Smithdown Road. Had the scientists got it wrong? Was this another earthquake? Pedestrians froze in horror as they watched a huge section of the tarmacadam on Smithdown Road give way, creating a massive hole. Fears that the city had been hit by another quake were, however, unfounded. The subsidence had ironically been caused by nothing more sinister than unusually heavy rains!

Britain is not immune from earthquakes, as we have seen. There are actually about two hundred every year, but only about twenty of these are detectable without special equipment. In 1101 the whole of England was shaken by a violent earthquake which was recorded by scribes across the land. One monk wrote that it was: "A horrid spectacle, for all the buildings were lifted up and then again settled as before."

In recent times, a tremor measuring 4.8 on the Richter Scale shook Liverpool and the rest of Merseyside just before 1am on 22 September 2002. The epicentre of the quake was in the Midlands, yet there were also many reports of slight structural damage across the North West.

Mighty Mary

Mary Richardson

On the Monday morning of 26 September 1921, doctors, sportsmen, military men and journalists from the Liverpool Echo assembled in the ballroom of the Adelphi Hotel. Among those gathered was one Captain Templeton, the governor of a French military prison and a martial arts expert who trained soldiers and the police in the art of self-defence. Standing alongside Templeton were six burly members of Liverpool Football Club and several muscular pugilists, all of whom had been invited to witness the strange and awesome powers of a Miss Mary Richardson, a petite, beautiful woman in her twenties. According to Templeton, Mary was possessed of some arcane power that enabled her to resist the efforts of a body of muscular men to lift, or move her in any way. Recently, Miss Richardson had single-handedly won a tug-of-war with a team of rugby players, and shamed weight-lifting champions who had tried in vain to raise her even a fraction of an inch above the ground.

The first task allotted to the six players from LFC was to try and push a billiard cue across Mary's palm – a seemingly easy enough task – but their twelve hands were unable to make the cue budge even the slightest bit. Afterwards, a team of doctors painstakingly analysed the lady's delicate palm, and failed to find any evidence of a deception. The six footballers, a strongman and an independent observer of the demonstration then attempted to lift the petite woman, but despite their best endeavours, Mary's dainty heels never left the carpet.

Harry Beadles – Liverpool FC's formidable outside left – threw open a window, gasping for air from his exertions. Later, poor Harry, having recovered from his earlier ordeals, unwisely raised his hand when Captain Templeton took centre stage and asked for a volunteer to help him demonstrate the deadly art of Katsu. He casually pressed his fingers on to Harry's neck and the footballer's head lolled forward, and his legs instantly gave way. Everybody in the audience gasped and then a deathly hush filled the ballroom. Had Templeton killed Beadles? The doctors quickly established that Harry had no pulse, but to everyone's relief, Templeton quickly revived him by manipulating the nerves in his collarbone.

When Harry was resuscitated he said that he had experienced a very strange form of deep unconsciousness when he was out cold, with no dreams and no sensation of his body. Colonel Templeton, explained the Katsu state of resuscitation to the medical men attending Beadles, and claimed that his techniques could save a person who was dying during an operation:

"By the exertion of pressure on the nervous centres in the region of the pectoral arch, dilation of the heart is induced. Simultaneously, a blow on the seventh dorsal vertebra causes the diaphragm to expand, drawing air into the lungs. Shouting at the patient will then stimulate the auditory nerves and assist in the rapid return to consciousness."

The immovable Mary Richardson and Captain Templeton later went onstage at the Olympia Theatre in West Derby Road and gave an even more astonishing performance. Two enormous dray-horses, loaned by a Mr Roberts, a local man, were brought on to the stage and their harnesses were tied to Mary's waist by a rope. The beasts of burden then laboured under their owner's whip to drag Miss Richardson from centre stage until the rope strained. The horses foamed at the mouth but Mary, without seeming to be straining or resisting them in any way, stayed exactly where she was. The genuinely astonished audience gave her a standing ovation.

Minutes later, thirteen men, including most of the LFC team, lined up on one side of Mary, while a respected doctor, and a psychical researcher named Holms, rested their hands on her shoulders. The signal was given, and the thirteen men collectively pushed against 'Mighty Mary' – yet she never budged an inch, and the doctor and Mr Holms could not detect any force being exerted on the woman's body.

After the demonstration, Mary lightly touched one of the footballers and he was knocked clean across the stage by an invisible force.

Mighty Mary later vanished into obscurity, and it still has not been established how she performed her superhuman feats of strength.

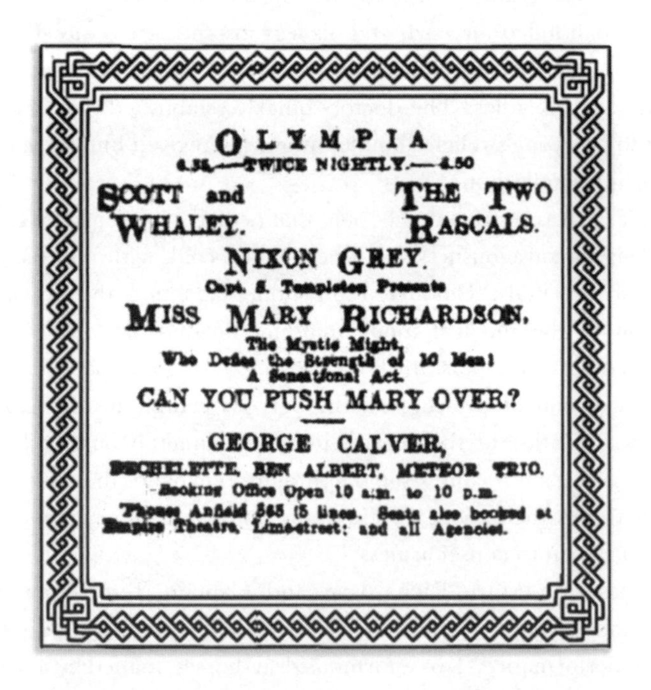

The Mothak Aircrash Mystery

Mothak Aircrash

On Tuesday 20 July 1965, at 6.17pm, sixty-eight-year-old Edward Harrison, forecourt attendant at Haggis' Garage on Speke Road, had just finished checking a customer's oil and was lowering the car's bonnet when he heard the unusual low moan of a plane coming from somewhere in the sky behind his filling station. He looked up and watched as the aircraft glided past him overhead in the murky yellow sky. The plane was so low that Harrison was worried that its undercarriage was going to clip the top of the lamp-post on the opposite side of the road. It was a scene straight out of a nightmare. The pilot was obviously struggling to pull the nose up to gain height, but despite the intense revving of the turbo-prop's four-engines, the plane banked steadily to the right, losing momentum, and a heartbeat later the Viscount aircraft plunged downwards – seemingly in slow motion – towards Thompson and Capper's factory complex; a place stocked with highly inflammable liquids and other combustible chemicals. Harrison was so shocked that he was rooted to the spot for a while, and when he finally regained his senses he rushed to the telephone and dialled 999.

Meanwhile, on the perimeter road of the industrial area, near to the Ford Factory, a Liverpool University dental student named Peter Hartles was driving home to Widnes when he also noticed the chilling sight of Viscount Oscar Lima making its breathtaking plunge into the factory. Seconds before he had been watching the plane and had assumed it was coming in to land at Speke Airport. Then he noticed that the Viscount had apparently overshot Runway 26. The visibility at this time was about a mile and all the lights on the runway were fully operational. Although it was July, the area was shrouded with drizzling rain and patches of mist.

There were other eye-witnesses to the unfolding disaster, such as fifteen-year-old Graham Bishop. He was talking to a friend on his doorstep on nearby Dymchurch Road when the two youths were startled by the very low approach of the Viscount flying over their heads, almost at rooftop level. Graham later told Roy Corlett of the Liverpool Echo: "The plane sloped over to one side, and as it was going over the factory, it suddenly crashed on to the building with a loud bang. Flames and smoke poured out of it."

Garston butcher Jack Fenelon, meanwhile, was driving along Speke Road when he saw a tremendous flash of light from the direction of the Mothak Factory – the sixty-three-seater plane had crashed into it. Fenelon drove further down Speke Road and gradually realised that the flash of light had originated from a point right in the centre of the factory where huge flames were now erupting into the sky. Then the butcher saw the sickening sight of the tail-plane of the Viscount sticking up in the midst of the flames and clouds of billowing smoke.

At Speke Airport, a British Eagle Britannia plane waited at the end of the taxi-way of Runway 26 – where the Viscount had been intending to touch down. The Britannia was all set to make a return trip to London when the disaster took place, but it would now have its flight postponed. Miles away, over the Irish Sea, an incoming Aer Lingus aeroplane on its way from Dublin to Liverpool had to be diverted to Manchester because of the huge, thick black clouds of smoke obscuring the runways.

Mr Gordon Griffiths, forty-year-old director of Thompson and Capper Ltd, was working in his office, less than fifty yards from the point of impact. He survived and later told reporters: "I heard the plane coming in very low over the building. I had a premonition there would be a crash, and there was a terrific noise that shook the whole building. I ran towards the source of the explosion and found that the whole centre of the building was enveloped in flames."

Thankfully, just forty-five minutes earlier, most of the 280 employees at the Speke factory had gone home, but now the Mothak's room, where mothballs and fertiliser were manufactured using naphthalene and methylated spirit, was a raging inferno. At first, no one was sure if any of the employees had stayed behind at the Mothak's room to work overtime, but sadly it soon became apparent that some of them had, and had lost their lives as a result. Three young women, Carol Barrett, aged twenty, of Lovel Road, Speke, her friend, seventeen-year-old Laura Hill of Garston, and sixteen-year-old Helen Stewart of East Millwood Road, Speke, missed death by seconds. Two of these girls were working overtime in the packing room, while a third was gazing idly out of a window when she saw the terrifying sight of the plane heading straight towards the factory. The girl screamed to her friends to get out as fast as they could and they just managed to get clear of the building in time, seconds before the impact and resulting deadly fireball. Ben Blacklock, a warehouse foreman at the factory, also narrowly escaped death by smashing a window and jumping to safety as the Viscount careered down out of the sky.

Mrs June Eira Stimpson, aged twenty-three, of Hughestead Grove, Garston, was not so lucky. Neither was her forty-six-year-old friend, Miss Elizabeth Farrell, of Aigburth Drive. The two factory supervisors had chosen to work overtime that day, and both perished in the crash and ensuing inferno. Mrs Stimpson had been married for just one year, and her husband Frederick, was naturally devastated when he learned of her tragic death. The other victim, Miss Farrell, had been making regular visits to her brother who was ill in hospital, and it had been her intention to visit him after work at the factory on the fateful day of the crash. A member of the dead woman's family said, "We dare not tell her brother what has happened to her, as he is still on the danger list, but he will soon be asking why she is not visiting him, and what we will tell him? I don't yet know."

The Viscount aircraft had been piloted by Captain Mike Warrington, aged thirty-nine, of Rhoose in Cardiff. Captain Warrington and his First Officer, twenty-seven-year-old Peter Kenney of Cartfield Road, Liverpool, were ex-RAF pilots and both men died in the crash. Cambrian Airways owned the Viscount and employed all her crew. Captain Warrington was a married man with two children and had lived close to Cardiff Airport in Porthkerry Road, Rhoose. He had been with Cambrian Airways for three years and notched up 8000 hours of flying time with the company. Peter Kenney had lived the last five months of his life at Rodney House on Parkfield Road, near to Sefton Park. Residents there remembered him as a cheerful, friendly young man who was never too busy to stop for a chat. He had only one known relative, an aunt who lived in Wimbledon, where his girlfriend also resided.

Earlier on that day when the two men tragically lost their lives, they had left Liverpool at 9am, taking holiday-makers to Jersey and bringing another group home. The seats of the aircraft were then removed as the crew lunched at Speke, and at 2.45pm, the Viscount took off for the Isle of Man with a cargo of mixed freight. The plane left the island for the ill-fated return trip at 5.30pm – the last flight of the day. At eight minutes past six it passed over Wallasey beacon and appeared as a blip on the radar screen at Speke Airport. However, seconds from what should have been a textbook touchdown on Runway 26, something went disastrously wrong. All of the eyewitness reports from those in the vicinity of the airport agreed that the Viscount was several hundred yards off course. All agreed that the plane's engines revved up but that it still lost altitude and banked to the right before turning on its back and impacting into the factory.

Enquiries and investigations into the crash went on for months, and mechanical error was mooted as the most likely cause, but there was no black box recorder on that plane and so no one knows what really happened. In Parliament, the Minister of Aviation, Roy Jenkins, told Eric Heiffer of the Opposition, that a full-scale enquiry would be held, but the causes of the Viscount Oscar Lima disaster remain shrouded in mystery. Human error was very unlikely as Captain Warrington was a respected and accomplished pilot with immense experience in the handling of such aircraft.

The actions of rescue workers and personnel of the fire and ambulance services in the wake of the crash were heroic. A twenty-three-year-old RAF airman on leave named Christopher Maideley had been on a bus passing the scene of the crash. He hurried from the vehicle and made a beeline for the blazing factory. Maideley was joined by firemen, who tore at the wreckage of the blazing plane with metal cutters and even their bare hands. Maideley showed the rescuers how to move back the seats in the cockpit in order to remove the Captain and the First Officer, but the men were already too badly burned and lifeless. Maideley and the firemen did manage to salvage documents and fragmented instrument panels which would hopefully enable the crash investigators to determine what had caused the plane to dive into the factory.

On the other side of the heap of twisted metal and incandescent rubble, Neil Birrell, the driver of a lorry, left his vehicle on Speke Hall Road and attempted to get to the plane but the intense heat kept him and other rescuers at bay. It soon became apparent that the fire was not just the result of the plane's ruptured fuel tank and the highly combustible chemicals at the plant; a fractured, two-inch-diameter gas main was also feeding the flames. Over a hundred fire-fighters soon arrived upon the scene and sixteen fire appliances were deployed to control the blaze. It was not possible for the bodies of the women who died at the factory to be removed for almost ninety minutes because of the extent and intensity of the blaze.

Housewives on the corporation housing estate adjacent to Liverpool Airport told a team of newspaper journalists that they had lived in fear of such a plane crash for many years. Mrs Elizabeth O'Connor of Woodend Lane on the estate said she thought the planes always flew too low over the neighbourhood, and she had frequently said that it was just a matter of time before such a tragedy took place. Mrs Emma Owen of Rycroft Road agreed. She told a reporter: "I have dreaded this sort of thing happening. My husband has often predicted that such a terrible disaster would happen at the airport."

The Wavertree Coat

The Coffee House, Wavertree

Some of the greatest wagers, challenges and dares have been laid in Liverpool pubs, yet many Liverpool folk – usually teetotal people – pour scorn on what is known as 'ale talk'. It certainly is true that under the influence of beer, lager and spirits, the drinker is much more susceptible to flights of fancy and the hatching of unrealistic ideas. Manifestos for a utopian republic have been written on the back of beer mats, and many a pub genius has chalked, upon the darts scoreboard, the details of an invention that will make him an overnight millionaire. Unfortunately, when the effects of the Guinness wear off, the life-changing plans and ideas are seen to have fatal flaws.

However, not all ale talk is hollow. The fabulous tale of the Wavertree Coat began as a challenge in the Coffee House tavern in the blazing summer of 1905. Mr Thomas Tweddle, junior manager of the local High Street bank, was quaffing a draught of ale at the Coffee House as he watched the pub's two well-known argumentative customers challenging each other to ever more ludicrous dares. The pair were known as 'The Two Arthurs' – Arthur Fisher, a gasfitter, and Arthur Green, a clerk of works.

"Now, I bet you tuppence you cannot lift that stool up by the end of one of its legs, using just one hand," Green challenged Fisher, and the latter proved him wrong.

"Now, Arthur," said Arthur Fisher, stabbing his index finger into his namesake's barrel chest, "I bet you can't walk around the Roundhouse of Wavertree Green on your hands … I can."

Then Mr Tweddle interposed, "Now, now, gentleman, let's have less of this silly talk. Here's a real challenge for you, and I will pay three hundred English pounds to the man who proves me wrong."

A silence descended at the mention of such an enormous sum of money. An old drinker aimed his ear trumpet at the bank employee – this would be worth listening to!

"This jacket I wear, is of the purest wool fibre," said Tweddle, placing his thumbs under the lapels and twiddling his fingers. "If any person here can make such a coat between sunrise and sunset on a summer's day, from wool taken from the coat of sheep, I will pay him the sum of three hundred pounds."

"Impossible!" said the landlord of the Coffee House.

"Can't be done," agreed Arthur Green.

Heads were shaken throughout the pub – the general consensus was that it was completely unachievable.

However, Arthur Fisher thought long and hard about the challenge, but eventually said that he was definitely interested but that he didn't have anything like enough money to accept the wager. Tweddle was undeterred and said that Fisher's poor, unsuspecting girlfriend, sixteen-year-old Florence Murray, would suffice as payment, if he failed to meet the challenge. Incredibly, because Fisher was drunk, he accepted the wager, and even more incredibly, Florence's father, who was also one of the coffee House regulars, gave his permission as well, adding that Tweddle would make an excellent son-in-law!

It was agreed that Saturday, 12 August was the day on which the coat had to be made. Arthur Fisher enlisted all the help he could get to assist him in the task. Old Farmer Jackson of Childwall would provide two sheep, Mr Gill, a local headmaster, claimed he had female relatives in Huyton who had old, but functional spinning wheels to spin the wool into yarn and looms on which to weave it into fabric. Local sartorial wizard with needle and thread, Isaac Nieman, would be the tailor. News of the challenge spread fast and a Mr Aitken, the local chemist, joined in the challenge and promised that he would provide the black fabric dye for the coat. Several other local people also offered their help in return for some small part of the three hundred pound pay out. Mr Tweddle insisted on scrutinising every part of the procedure to rule out fraud.

Just before five o'clock on the morning of 12 August, Farmer Jackson and a shepherd had two sheep shorn. A fascinated crowd stood in attendance. The fleeces were washed, stubbed, roved and then taken to the looms of two old sisters at a Huyton cottage. The wool was spun, the yarn spooled, warped, and woven. Then the cloth was burred, milled and rowed at the expert hands of the septuagenarian sisters. The chemist Aitken mixed his dye in a bowl as the weavers scoured, fulled, tented, raised and sheared the cloth to give it an acceptable finish. Aitken professionally dyed the long strip of fabric, and then hung it out to dry in the sun.

The minutes ticked by, meanwhile, and Arthur Fisher nervously bit his nails and paced about round his little army of workers. Three hours later, the bone-dry cloth was placed in the dextrous hands of Mr Nieman the tailor. However, when Nieman entered his tailor's shop, he discovered that the premises had been broken into, and as well as numerous bolts of cloth, practically all the tools of his trade had been stolen. Fortunately, a dressmaker named Mary Davies came to Mr Nieman's aid and not only did she lend the tailor her tools, but she also enlisted the help of four relations who were very accomplished with a needle and thread. By eight o'clock in the evening, the 'Wavertree Coat' was presented to Mr Tweddle, and it fitted him perfectly and the three hundred pounds was duly handed over in a gentlemanly manner to Arthur Fisher.

Ironically, young Florence Murray later fell for the charms of Tweddle, and deserted poor Arthur, despite his new-found wealth!

Wild Animals at Large in Liverpool

Escaped Bear

The tragedy unfolded on the Thursday morning of 24 March 1938, when Mickey the chimpanzee, adored by hundreds of Liverpool children, broke one of the inch-thick bars in his cage at the Liverpool Zoological Park at Rosemont Road, Aigburth, and made his escape by quickly squeezing through the gap. It was the chimp's fourth escape from the zoo, because Mickey was not at all happy being constantly at the centre of noisy crowds of onlookers who would surround him in his chain link enclosure. Many of them simply came to taunt and laugh at him as he hugged an old football for comfort and security. There was no way of hiding from his tormentors in his barren cage, the only way to get away from them was to escape.

The runaway chimp headed straight for the nearby house of the zoo's proprietor Mr Rogers and he used his Herculean strength to smash down the front door. In a highly agitated state, he then charged into the room of his closest human friend, Mrs Wardle. Mrs Wardle was one of the few people who could handle Mickey and tell him what to do, but upon this occasion she was unable to calm him down at all, and when she tried to restrain him, he slipped out of her grasp and ran outside. Mrs Wardle managed to catch up with him but Mickey, sensing that she was about to take away his new found freedom, pushed her roughly to the ground and savagely clawed her neck. He then bolted off again as Mrs Wardle's husband fetched a service rifle and raised the alarm.

Before the chimp had left the zoological park, an armed posse of zookeepers was on his trail and one of them fired at Mickey, wounding him. The poor creature wailed in agony and headed off towards nearby Sudley Road Council School – where a group of young pupils were standing in lines doing their exercises in the playground under the supervision of their class teacher, Mr Gall.

The children were startled by a terrified yelp and Mr Gall looked up to find the bloodied chimpanzee gripping one of his petrified pupils by the ankle. Mr Gall had encountered Mickey during one of his previous escapes and was only too well aware of his tremendous power, yet the teacher bravely confronted the animal to rescue his unfortunate pupil and protect the rest of the class. Gall was picked up and effortlessly hurled across the yard, and when he came to his senses on the asphalt, the chimp was still in the playground, circling round the terrified pupils making high-pitched shrieking sounds.

Moments afterwards Mickey lurched out of the school gates and headed off to a nearby street of terraced houses, where he climbed up a drainpipe on to one of the roofs with amazing agility and worked his way along the ridge tiles, going from house to house. He finally paused at the chimney stack of 29 Lugard Road, and gazed down at his pursuers with eyes that were wide with terror. A bullet whizzed through the air and winged him and he yelled out in agony, then he cowered behind the chimney pots, nursing his wounds.

A contingent of armed policemen scrambled into the back alleyways, and after a brief discussion, agreed that there was no alternative – the chimp was just too dangerous to be tackled, even in his wounded state. He was a threat to the public and had to be killed. Two more shots rang out and Mickey clutched at his throat and tumbled into the backyard of No 29. He crawled into a corner, bleeding profusely and whimpering pitifully. He used the last ounce of his strength to reach out for an old scuffed football lying in the yard; just like the one he had cherished at the zoo.

Major CJ Bailey of the 38th Anti-Aircraft Battalion arrived in a neighbouring yard and with his service rifle, he fired the two shots which ended Mickey's life.

Even in death the zoo's owners continued to exploit the poor creature. They had lost their major attraction and in order to keep up visitor numbers to the zoo they had Mickey stuffed and put on display. But Liverpool Zoo just wasn't the same without its simian star attraction, and it was forced to close later that year.

Mr Drew, the gardener at nearby High Pastures, had fond memories of Mickey the chimpanzee, and had, on previous occasions, managed to coax the troublesome creature back to the zoo. One morning Mickey had escaped and Mr Drew had gone off in search of him, only to find him sitting alongside the terrified driver of a lorry delivering coal to the Rosemount estate!

The Liverpool Zoo had been the scene of another tragedy shortly before the death of Mickey; a tragedy which started when thirty-five-year-old attendant, John Ashworth, was cleaning the cage of two of the zoo's leopards. Ashworth had managed to entice the male and female leopards into a special compartment in the cage using an animal carcass as bait, before sliding a safety partition between himself and the dangerous animals. After cleaning half of the cage he was supposed to leave it, then slide the partition back allowing the big cats to re-enter the cleaned half of their enclosure.

For some unknown reason, Ashworth instead called the leopards to come through into the half of the cage which he'd been cleaning, and didn't stay behind the safety partition. He probably felt confident that no harm would come to him as he had known both the leopards since birth, and he also held a whip with which to control them. But it was to prove to be a fatal mistake.

Things started to go horribly wrong when the male leopard darted past him and crouched tensely in the corner of the cage, teeth bared, as if ready to spring. Ashworth cracked his whip several times and the leopard shrank back into the corner emitting a low growl. The attendant then called to the female leopard and gestured for her to come through with his arm, but she hesitated, probably intimidated by the snarling male, and as Ashworth turned his back on the crouching male leopard to encourage her, it suddenly sprang at him from behind, knocking him sideways.

Ashworth and the leopard tumbled about in the cage in a deadly struggle during which the whip was forced from his hand and the big cat tore out parts of his throat. Horrified, Ashworth felt the deep gaping bite wounds in his neck and started to cough and splutter as blood poured down his throat. Eventually, the keeper desperately grabbed hold of his mop and managed to keep the cat at bay just long enough to get back into the safety of the other half of the cage. By now his face had taken on a deathly pallor and he was visibly bleeding to death. With the disappointed roars of the ferocious leopard still ringing in his ears, he somehow managed to stumble out of the cage with arterial blood spraying high into the air. Then he collapsed.

An ambulance was quickly in attendance and it raced to Smithdown Road Hospital, bells ringing, but John Ashworth was certified dead on arrival; he had bled to death in a matter of minutes.

Shortly before Ashworth was fatally mauled, one hundred and fifty school children had gathered around the caged leopards before going to see a circus performance at the other end of the zoo. Fortunately, none of them had been aware of the tragedy which followed.

In Victorian times Liverpudlian lives were imperilled by escaped animals from menageries and zoos on numerous occasions, with two very serious incidents taking place in the mid-1880s.

In Kensington, on Monday 28 July 1884, a large herd of oxen was being driven to town from Stanley Cattle Market, on their way to meet their fate at the abattoir. The lumbering procession of beasts was always regarded as a spectacle by the townspeople of Kensington, but on this hot summer morning, another parade of animals, of a far more exotic nature than mere oxen, was also traversing the streets; animals which no local person had ever seen before, but perhaps only read of in the Bible. They were being brought to Kensington Fields to be sold at auction. The animals were collectively known by the unlikely title of the famous Edmonds-Wombwell Royal Windsor Castle (Travelling) Menagerie.

Children gasped in wonder at the sight of a horse and a camel harnessed side by side, pulling a caravan, followed a massive bear, some giraffes, an over-sized, muscular, forest-bred lion named Wallace, a hamadryad (a large Arabian baboon held sacred by the ancient Egyptians) and, most spectacular of all amongst the pageant of one hundred and twenty-seven outlandish animals, was a truly massive, eighteen-year-old African elephant named Emperor, who measured eleven feet in height.

It was while Emperor was engaged in moving a caravan at Kensington Fields that a grave mishap took place. The elephant suddenly bolted – with its driver still on its back – and burst out of the flimsy enclosure. It thundered on to the main road sending terrified people scattering in every direction. Emperor careered down Kensington High Street, its great, bulbous feet crushing all the carefully-arranged merchandise displayed outside the numerous shops. The keeper clinging to the elephant's back for dear life repeatedly screamed for him to stop, but Emperor was much too busy enjoying his new-found freedom to pay any heed.

Suddenly, the elephant's massive trunk snaked upwards and rose high into the air as the beast emitted a triumphant trumpeting sound. The elephant then reared back, standing momentarily on two of its four tree trunk-thick legs. Then, with all four feet back on the ground, it charged towards the herd of oxen which were still ambling peacefully along some distance away, unaware of the commotion at the other end of the street. The keeper clinging on to Emperor's back knew that many of the oxen would be crushed to death by the giant African elephant unless he could somehow manage to persuade it to swerve away from them.

"Emperor! Whoa!" he cried into one of the huge flapping ears, and, to his relief, the elephant immediately responded by slowing down and changing direction. He made a right-angle turn and started trotting towards a public house. For a few tense moments Emperor seemed transfixed by his own reflection in the plate glass window of the pub and he came to a halt. Just when the keeper thought that the crisis was over, Emperor's trunk went up again and with a trumpeting roar, he charged straight at the pub. Mrs Winthrop and Mr Beaumont, two well known drunks who had been drinking in the pub since it had opened its doors that morning, stared in disbelief and horror at the surreal sight of the gigantic elephant's head, tusks and all, now thundering towards the pub window. Through some miracle, the man on the elephant's back managed to stop the beast in its tracks in the nick of time. Mrs Winthrop passed out and had to be revived with brandy.

Not long after that incident, an enormous brown bear from the same menagerie made its escape and prowled the streets of Kensington, walking mostly on its hind legs, giving it a towering stature of almost seven feet, and adding to its intimidating appearance. A young man who was known locally as a tough street fighter, foolishly attempted to tackle the bear while most people with any sense had already run for cover and bolted themselves inside the nearest building.

Not surprisingly, the man was severely mauled by the bear, which ripped off strips of muscle and skin from his arm with its massive claws. The arm was so badly lacerated that it later had to be amputated, but the brave, if foolhardy, youth did succeed in luring the menacing creature into a corner, where a gang of men wielding pick-axe handles and nets were finally able to restrain and recapture it.

The one-armed, have-a-go hero later bought a pub and called it The Bear, and apparently did a roaring trade. People from miles around came to sup their ale at the pub and hear the famous publican relate his account of his courageous encounter with the seven-foot bear.

Perhaps the most bizarre occurrence concerning a wild animal at large in Liverpool took place in August 1971, when a large, perfect specimen of a stag was spotted running down the streets of the city. Police set up road blocks and sent out patrols to recapture the out-of-place animal, but before they could put their plan into action, the stag met its tragic end when it was knocked down by a car in North John Street. Its injuries were so appalling that a vet had to be called to put it out of its misery.

How a wild deer came to be at large in Liverpool city centre has never been explained. Had rustlers taken the stag from some rural area and put it in the back of a van or lorry, and had the animal then escaped from the vehicle whilst it was in transit through the city? We can only speculate, but the truth will probably never be known.

The Life of Riley

In the pantheon of outstanding Liverpool characters, many local names have achieved world-wide fame, usually either through hard work and dogged persistence, or sheer natural ability or talent, but one Liverpudlian legend – Michael Riley – became world renowned through making a career out of idleness, of doing absolutely nothing. He survived solely on his natural charm and the luck of the Irish.

Mick Riley was said to have been one of the eleven children born to a family living in an overcrowded house on Scotland Road in the 1870s. All of the Rileys were known in the community as honest, hardworking folk, all except for young Mick, that is, whose bone idleness was a constant bone of contention in the Riley household. He was invariably the last to rise from his bed in the morning, and he usually took the line of least resistance when it came to making a living for himself, or contributing in any way to the family's income. Mick had a phobia of hard work, and often resorted to theft and deception in an effort to compete financially with his eight law-abiding brothers (all of them navvies) and highly principled twin sisters.

Although he was undoubtedly the black sheep of the family, Mick was blessed with a charmer's tongue and a likeable, comical face that could melt the fiercest heart and he was therefore still popular with both friends and family, despite his considerable shortcomings.

When Mick was just twelve years old, local innkeeper Jesse Turner reported the theft of one of his gigantic Jersey cabbages from his garden. The policeman investigating the unusual case, initially doubted the accuracy of Turner's description of the prize cabbage as being approximately six feet in height – until young Riley and his slow-witted accomplice were apprehended struggling to convey the mammoth vegetable away from the scene of the crime on a small handcart. Publican Jesse Turner, an eccentric individual who had appropriately called his inn, Cabbage Hall, having retrieved his prize cabbage, decided not to press charges against the young scallywag Riley and his hapless mate, deeming the theft to be nothing more than a childish prank. He even went on to hire Riley for a while as a messenger boy – until Riley absconded with some of his money, that is.

Riley, at thirteen, was finally disowned by his disgraced parents after he broke into a local confectioner's shop and ate so many cakes that he made himself sick. One of his uncles, who was in the army, hearing of the lad's latest exploit, took pity on his long-suffering parents and offered to take young Riley under his wing, promising to "make a man of him" in the army. But the barefoot sloth had other ideas about his destiny, and when he caught wind of the scheme, he ran away from Scotland Road as fast as his legs could carry him. For a while he had been thinking about his future– specifically how to get rich quick without breaking into a sweat – and he had decided that a life on the ocean waves was the one for him and so he made his way to Liverpool Docks, like so many youngsters before him.

Never one to choose the legitimate route, Mick Riley managed to sneak onboard the City of Brussels transatlantic passenger liner bound for New York, and soon found himself a comfortable enough billet behind some flour sacks deep inside the hold and settled himself down for the long, trans-Atlantic voyage. However, as soon as the ship set sail, he began to feel very hungry and thirsty – in his haste to leave home undetected, he had come on board with no provisions to see him through the voyage. He realised that he would sooner or later have to locate the ship's kitchens and find himself something to eat and drink, or he would starve to death.

So, late that night, when the ship went quiet, Riley crept out of his hiding place in the hold and set off to forage for food. He had never been on a ship before and had no idea where the kitchens might be located. He searched high and low, going up and down from deck to deck, and had several narrow escapes when he came across sailors on watch, or passengers who could not sleep and had decided to walk about the decks taking the sea air. However, he managed to stay out of sight by keeping to the shadows and eventually located the kitchens which were in semi-darkness, the kitchen staff having finished for the night.

The first thing he did was to help himself to a large glass of water as he was even thirstier than he was hungry – probably due to the salt air. Then he started to explore the vast store cupboards. Ocean going liners in those days were like vast, sumptuous, floating hotels, offering every conceivable kind of delicacy to their first class passengers and it was not long before he was tucking into exotic foods the like of which he had never tasted before in his life: lobster, salmon, delicious hams and the most exquisite fruits and pastries. With one hand he crammed food into his mouth and with the other he stuffed it into his pockets, realising that it might be a long time before he could sneak out again for his next meal. He was in imminent danger of making himself sick yet again, when he heard a noise which sounded like someone approaching. Gulping down an enormous piece of chocolate torte, he quickly stepped behind a tall store cupboard. The footsteps came nearer. Out of the darkness came a stern man's voice.

"Come out at once. You can't hide from me, boy. I know you're in there."

Captain Land, in the course of one of his routine inspections of the ship, had caught sight of the young scoundrel sneaking about the kitchens, stuffing vast quantities of food into his mouth. He marched up to the cupboard and yanked Mick Riley out by his ear.

"Aha! A young stowaway, I'll be bound. It's off to the lock-up with you, my lad, and you'll get a jolly good thrashing in the morning."

" But sir, sir ..."

There was no arguing with Captain Land and Riley was soon locked away in a room for the rest of the night, but at least he now had a full stomach, and it was quite warm in the room. Even with the threat of a severe thrashing hanging over him, the ever cheerful Riley was soon sleeping like a baby, dreaming of the exciting adventures he expected to have once they arrived in New York.

The next morning, fortune smiled once again on the amiable Liverpool stray when the captain heard him singing an old Irish ballad. He had a beautiful voice which might have earned him a place as a choirboy had he been born into more fortunate circumstances. Captain Land's grandmother had often sung that particular song to him when he was a child, and hearing the lilting strains being sung so innocently brought back a flood of touching memories. The captain was overcome with emotion and embraced the astonished Riley as if he were his own son. He then summoned the ship's cook and ordered him to serve the lad a hot meal.

Mick Riley was given a new outfit of smart clothes, including shoes and socks, which felt most peculiar at first as he had never worn them before in his life. Throughout the voyage, he entertained the passengers and crew with his vast repertoire of Irish songs, as well as his seemingly never-ending supply of stories from his home town. He was allocated sleeping quarters with the crew, who were equally taken with him and he enjoyed better food than he had ever had in his life.

When the ship finally docked at New York, Riley was quite disappointed that the voyage had come to an end, because he was having such a wonderful time, but he was in for yet another piece of good luck. Just as he was about to disembark, he was taken to one side by a wealthy family who were travelling to join the rest of their relations in the American Deep South. They, like all the other passengers, had been utterly captivated by the boy's charms and the angelic quality of his voice and they told Mick that they wanted to adopt him into their family. Mick Riley jumped at the opportunity and soon found himself living with his adoptive family in the lap of luxury in a beautiful old house. He could always be found, in the lazy heat of the afternoons, snoozing on one of the verandahs which surrounded the property.

Riley married a beautiful, rich, southern belle when he reached the age of fifteen and she mollycoddled and cosseted him from morning till night. He spent the remainder of his life as a blissful layabout who rose at noon each day, spent long, lazy afternoons fishing or languidly loafing about the plantation and long, hot, sultry nights soaking up enormous quantities of bourbon, as he gambled away his wife's fortune at the card tables. It was a life to which he was eminently suited – there was no longer any question of searching for anything better – his destiny had been fulfilled.

Michael Riley soon became a colourful local legend and Vaudeville crooners were soon singing about 'the life of Riley' and unknowingly coined a popular phrase that soon travelled the world and is still in popular use today, meaning someone who manages to get away with doing nothing, while still enjoying the best of everything.

Dashing Dan of Lime Street

Dashing Dan

In the 1890s, Danby Gifford, an eccentric but well-intentioned character of some distinction, cut a well-known figure on the streets of Liverpool. An incurable insomniac, Danby, or 'Dashing Dan' as he was known, would leave the security of the three hundred and eighty-roomed North Western Hotel on Lime Street each night, and patrol the midnight streets, armed with a silver, gilt-handled, malacca sword stick and a .22-calibre, two-shot Derringer. He claimed that the pistol was the very same one with which Wilkes shot President Lincoln. He said that it had been won from a riverboat gambler in the American Deep South.

At midnight, on 16 August 1894, a full moon hung over Lime Street. Dan Gifford passed the hotel receptionist – who was busy in conversation with a young inebriated female guest – and strolled out of the lobby and into the moonlit thoroughfare, in search of adventure. With his silk top hat, flowing, satin-lined cape and twirling swordstick, Gifford presented an impressive sight to any citizens of Liverpool who were still abroad at that hour. His snowy-white, waxed moustache, ostentatiously turned up and twisted into finely tapered ends, and his silver, bejewelled tie-pin, gave him the air of someone of importance; perhaps a retired brigadier, or maybe a judge. Even at that late hour, Lime Street was still busy with scurrying hansom cabs and people coming out of the train station. The Empire Theatre had long since emptied out its crowd and a lone actor was just leaving by the stage door. Outside the Legs of Man public house, a gaudily dressed lady of the night sidled up to Mr Gifford and propositioned him. He became incensed at the very idea and turned purple with indignation. Waving his swordstick aloft, Gifford addressed the young prostitute.

"How dare you, madam! I am a respectable gentleman," he growled. "Away with you at once."

The petite blonde streetwalker was completely unabashed – she'd heard it all before and any comment, no matter how disparaging, was like water off a duck's back to her. She folded her arms defiantly and grinned mockingly straight into his wild blue eyes.

"Alright, grandpa, don't take it personal. I never asked for your hand in marriage," she said, then minced off towards a staggering sailor on London Road, ready to waylay him with her feminine charms.

"The wages of sin is death!" Gifford called after her, then crossed over to St George's Plateau, still tutting to himself and feeling highly offended.

The top-hatted knight was going in search of damsels in distress, whom he could rescue from a fate worse than death – he was not interested in some brazen, scarlet slut who was after his money and his morals. He detested such low-life specimens of kerbstone Liverpool and regarded them as a plague on the city.

Just then two young, shabbily dressed men in flat caps leapt out from behind the base of one of the four enormous lion statues in front of St George's Hall. One of them was holding a cosh and Gifford immediately realised that he was in grave danger.

"If you shout, I'll break your bleedin' skull, old man," said one of the delinquents, while the other roughly grabbed hold of Gifford's arm and pinned it behind his back.

The old man drew his sword from its scabbard in an instant and swung its shimmering blade at the cosh-wielding youth with such ferocity that sparks flew off its tip when it struck the statue's granite plinth. The youth holding Gifford's arm received a nasty kick to his groin, but at the same moment, the other mugger struck Gifford's forehead.

"Curse you, you damned blackguards!" shouted Gifford, as he staggered backwards in a daze, with his back to the huge silhouetted hulk of St George's Hall. At least he still had his trusty sword, and he retreated backwards up the stairs as the two thugs closed in on him. The blow to his head had affected his sense of balance and he began to sway as he fumbled in his coat pocket for the Derringer pistol, but he couldn't find it. The two young ruffians rushed up the steps towards Gifford and he watched helplessly, as one of them raised the cosh, ready to dash it down on to his head, but, at the last moment, his assailant suddenly hesitated and turned around.

The blonde streetwalker who had approached Gifford earlier was rushing up the steps screaming a string of profanities at the two men, and one of them immediately ran away down the steps. The remaining attacker was suddenly floored with a powerful uppercut to his chin from the heroic little woman. The prostitute then knelt down beside Gifford, and, after telling him he shouldn't have been walking about so late on his own, she produced a handkerchief and dabbed his grazed forehead. She then insisted on accompanying him back to his hotel and seeing him safely inside before vanishing back into the night.

Dashing Dan's attitude towards Liverpool's street women underwent a dramatic change as a result of that night's adventures and the heroic actions of the plucky prostitute. He was determined to make amends for his initial rudeness and also wanted to show his gratitude to her for rescuing him from a highly dangerous situation. After making extensive enquiries about her identity, he learned that her name was Maggie May and that she lived on Mann Street. He sought out the dingy hovel that she called home and found her living in the direst poverty with her two ragged young children. It was obvious that she was struggling to feed and clothe her offspring. Gifford handed her a considerable amount of money as a reward for saving his life, and Maggie was tearfully thankful.

"No, my dear. It is I who should be thanking you," protested Gifford. "You saved my life even though I had been appallingly rude to you."

Was this woman the fabled Maggie May so often sung about in sailor's ballads, or merely her namesake?

Dashing Dan of Lime Street was involved in many adventures in Victorian and Edwardian Liverpool, and the silvery-haired crusader's escapades could fill a book on their own. One day I will relate more tales of this long-forgotten character of bygone Liverpool.

The King of Everton

Owen Elias

It's strange how we rarely give a second thought to the origin of the names behind our streets, squares, roads and avenues in Liverpool.

Living in Edge Hill, in my youth, I never wondered who the elegant Abercromby Square might have been named after, but I now know that the Georgian square was actually built in commemoration of General Sir Ralph Abercromby (1734-1801), the Commander of the British Army out in Egypt, who was killed in action in 1801 at the battle of Alexandria.

How many of us passing through Catherine Street have ever pondered on just who Catherine was? Well, apparently she was the mother of architect and builder William Jones (1788-1876), who built his own home at 35 Catherine Street.

Some street names have changed over the course of time through distorted pronunciation. Ullet Road, for example, in the postal areas of Liverpool 8 and 17, was originally called Owlet Road.

Subtly encoded in over twenty streets names in Walton is the name of a long-forgotten firm of Welsh builders – Owen and William Owen Elias. The first letters of the street names spell out the firm, and these streets – most of them linking County and Goodison Roads – are: Oxton, Winslow, Eton, Neston, Andrew, Nimrod, Dane, Wilburn, Ismay, Lind, Lowell, Index, Arnot, Makin, Olney, Weldon, Euston, Nixon, Eton, Liston, Imrie, Aston and Stuart (Road).

The firm behind the construction of these streets and many other construction projects in Everton was a deeply religious man of short stature, named Owen Elias. Owen was born in the parish of Llanbadrig on the Isle of Angelsey in 1806. As a youth he was apprenticed to a village joiner in Llanfechell, where he became religiously inspired to develop a grand ambition in life by the sermons of a local preacher. Owen realised that he could never realise his ambitions within the confines of Angelsey and he resolved to leave home at the age of nineteen. Having reached that age, he bid farewell to his friends and family and sailed in a small boat from Amlwch Harbour to the port of Liverpool, the promising destination of many a Welshman in search of fortune.

Owen had virtually no source of finance to back his dream of becoming a successful, self-employed builder, and possessed only the measly sum of eight shillings upon his arrival in Liverpool. His only real asset was a powerful will to succeed and he set about achieving his ambition through sheer hard work and determination. He accepted anything that was offered him and undertook employment in the lowliest jobs for the Corporation. Through a combination of thrift and sheer diligence, he eventually succeeded in turning his dream into a reality.

He teamed up with another poor worker by the name of Roberts and they decided to build a series of small, but well-built cottages for working men which they would rent out at three shillings and sixpence a week. The scheme worked well and Owen reinvested his profits into his cottage-building scheme, putting up properties in Kirkdale, Everton, Walton, West Derby, Toxteth Park and Cabbage Hall.

The money began to pour in from the rents, and Owen then embarked on the extensive erection of entire streets of houses on the hills of Everton, which at that time, was the 'Nob Hill' of Liverpool. It was the place to live if you were wealthy and noble, with its pure sea air blowing into its heights from the River Mersey, and the magnificent views of Liverpool Bay, North Wales and, of course, the river itself, which was perpetually bespecked with tall, canvas-sailed ships sailing to and fro on lucrative, if often hazardous, voyages to every corner of the globe.

Owen's massive construction projects, involving the building of hundreds of houses on the land between Great Homer Street and Heyworth Street, earned him the nickname of the 'King of Everton', and the Welsh 'Royal' resided at Mere House – a grand old mansion on Mere Lane at the time of his reign. After the construction of the streets that spelled out the name of his firm, Owen Elias took the sequence further to include spelling out the name of his eldest son, E. Alfred Owen.

Despite the accumulation of great wealth, Owen Elias remained a strictly religious man who also concerned himself with the construction of chapels and schools, and when he died on 31 January 1880, his personal estate was valued at around seventy thousand pounds – a huge sum of money in those days. What an achievement for a poor Welsh boy who had arrived in Liverpool with only eight shillings in his pocket!

Neston Street

Mysteries of Underground Liverpool

Liverpool has a thriving tourist industry nowadays. People from every corner of the globe flock to our city to embark on the Magical Mystery Tours of the old Beatles haunts, to admire Jesse Hartley's Gargantuan Albert Dock and the magnificent River Mersey, the museums and the art galleries, the two stunning cathedrals and numerous other civic attractions, but there is another potential tourist goldmine hidden right beneath our feet, as we are literally living in a 'double-decker' city. Most of us now know about the labyrinth of tunnels and vaults beneath Edge Hill, hewn out of the sandstone on the instructions of Joseph Williamson – the eccentric Mason Street Mole, Mole of Edge Hill – in the nineteenth century, but how many of us know about the many other subterranean intrigues of Liverpool?

Take the 'secret' Mersey Tunnel, for example. For centuries, rumours and claims have abounded that a four-mile, under-river tunnel runs from Bebington to Speke, created hundreds of years ago by the monks from Birkenhead Priory. In fact, legend has it that there were also two other tunnels leading from the priory, one of which ran to New Brighton's red rocks (called the 'Red Noses'), and the other to Stanlawe, or Ince.

One story states that when Henry VIII sent one of his commissioners to plunder the priory gold at Birkenhead during the Dissolution of the Monasteries, one of the monks managed to make his escape down the tunnel to Speke carrying a valuable plate and other holy treasures carefully concealed under the skirts of his flowing habit. Unfortunately, the monk never made it to Speke as he was killed by falling rubble in a cave-in in the tunnel under the river.

There are other secret tunnels in Wirral which you will never find mentioned in the local history guidebooks. For example, there is an extensive tunnel network and a sinister subterranean complex beneath Bidston Hill, but the entrances to this warren on Hoylake and Boundary Roads are now covered up. The tunnels and secret rooms beneath Bidston Hill were definitely not used as air-raid shelters in World War Two and no one seems to know when they were originally excavated, or for what purpose. There are similar mysterious tunnels under Holt Hill at Tranmere.

Another well-kept underground secret is the Anfield Cemetery catacombs, modelled on the underground burial chambers of St Sebastians in Rome. The Anfield Catacombs lie twenty-five feet beneath the ground in deep stone recesses, and contain very few bodies.

Many years ago the wife of a Russian nobleman lost her life whilst visiting Liverpool and he had her corpse interred in the catacombs, as it would have been very difficult to transport her body back to Russia before the days of refrigeration. The aristocrat promised the authorities in Liverpool that he would return before long to build a magnificent church in Anfield, dedicated to the memory of his beloved wife. However, when he returned to Russia, he soon remarried and quickly forgot about his former wife and her tomb and the grandiose promises he had made. The forgotten Russian lady's body still lies mouldering in the Liverpool catacombs to this day.

In October 1951, workmen excavating the foundations of the bomb-blitzed Corn Exchange in Brunswick Street came upon a series of strange, subterranean passages at a depth of some forty-six feet. The diggers began to explore the damp, cobwebbed passageways and came upon a walled, waterlogged chamber, which was twelve feet square. Numerous old maps were consulted, but none of them provided any information about the chamber and the network of secret passages radiating out from it. However, the general consensus amongst local historians was that the workmen had stumbled upon a dungeon where French prisoners, captured during the Napoleonic Wars, had once been detained and interrogated.

Not long after the discovery of the subterranean dungeon, staff at a nearby bank on Brunswick Street reported hearing the sound of singing voices and the faint, but unmistakable, rattle of chains. The ghostly sounds were usually heard in the late afternoon and seemed to originate from somewhere deep inside the bank's vaults.

At around this time a shop situated close to the bank was being modernised, and when one of the basement walls was demolished, a room containing a coffin was discovered. The walled-up room was not like a proper burial vault, and the well-preserved body of the man inside the coffin – dressed in expensive mid-Victorian clothes – was never identified. Weeks after the coffin had been taken to a local cemetery and reburied, staff at the shop were startled by the first of many appearances of a smiling, Dickensian-looking character with rosy cheeks. He sported a monocle, and wore a chequered suit and a high, stiff, white collar. Even when the mysterious gentleman was not making one of his appearances, he was often to be heard laughing and singing eerily somewhere just out of sight.

The most intriguing haunting in this part of the city is the strange man in black who haunts Derby Square, and is believed to be a phantom who dates back to mediaeval times, when Liverpool Castle stood on the spot where the Victoria monument is now located.

In the early 1980s, when workmen were excavating Derby Square in preparation for the laying of the foundations for the Queen Elizabeth II Law Courts, a startling and rather gruesome discovery was made. A fully preserved, clothed and helmeted man – believed to have been a Roundhead soldier from the troubled times of the English Civil War – was found in the clay surrounding the last vestiges of Liverpool Castle's dungeons.

Within an hour of the discovery, a group of mysterious but official-looking people who claimed that they were from Liverpool University, turned up at the building site and took possession of the seventeenth century corpse, claiming that they were taking it away for research purposes. The body was very carefully removed from the clay, then placed in a coffin-like box, and whisked away in an unmarked van.

Some time later, when a local historian made enquiries at Liverpool University's archaeology department, he learned, to his dismay, that no one from the university knew anything about the find in Derby Square, and the whereabouts of the helmeted soldier are still unknown to this day. Had the body been reported to the coroner, as it should have been, all construction work on the new courts would have been suspended for many months whilst further excavations of the site were carried out. Was this perhaps why the body was removed and hidden without trace?

In 2002, a Mrs Williams sent me a copy of what is alleged to be a photograph of the Derby Square Roundhead, along with a letter describing the background to the intriguing photograph.

Most Liverpool people don't know where Roscoe Place is, but they will probably have walked past it many times. It is a short cul-de-sac at the top of Bold Street, and was once the only access to a highly secret underground club of sorts, which was frequented by members of Liverpool's criminal fraternity in the 1880s. They say that there is no honour among thieves, yet the crooks who used 'Griffin's' subterranean den were extremely loyal to one another. Any villain who had been initiated into the secret social establishment founded by Arthur Griffin, one of Lancashire's most notorious receivers of stolen goods, faced execution if he revealed the existence of the club, which even included PC Richard Reeves, 281, amongst its members. Reeves was a corrupt officer of the law who had a beat which encompassed Bold Street.

To gain access to Griffin's, you walked down Roscoe Place (ideally after dark) and, after checking you weren't being followed, turned down an alleyway, off which there was a heavy green wooden door containing a spy-hole. To gain entry, the member had to give a special knock and utter a password. He was then admitted into a house with a cellar that gave direct access to the underworld club. The permanently gas-lit, cloak-and-dagger bolt-hole – parts of which extended beneath Renshaw Street – had its own kitchen and a lounge, and was stocked with such luxuries as a wine cellar and a stockpile of (presumably stolen) beer barrels. The existence of Griffin's club was finally betrayed in an ironic twist of fate.

One sunny afternoon in 1886, master mariner Alfred Clanchy was drinking ale in an Everton pub called The Cheerful Horn when he overheard two men discussing the possibility of breaking into the strong room of a bank. One of the men was aged about fifty or more, and had a very distinctive appearance; he had a hawk nose, smoked a clay pipe and wore an ear-ring, whilst the other schemer was a small, smartly attired, chubby-faced youth of about eighteen. The delinquent and his crooked mentor, having finished their pints of ale, soon left the pub and vanished into the kaleidoscopic bustle of the streets of Victorian Liverpool.

Clanchy stood in the doorway of the pub nursing his mug of stout and happened to mention the outrageous conversation to a fellow drinker, along with a description of the two men, who seemed to have been strangers in the neighbourhood. Perhaps it was a police informer who finally passed on the very basic details of the bank job to a police constable, because the matter was soon reported to detectives, but when they interviewed Clanchy they dismissed his story as pure fiction.

However, about a month later, a gang of four men – including the couple Alfred Clanchy had overheard discussing their stratagems in the Everton pub – managed to tunnel their way using pickaxes, sledgehammers and long chisels from the cellar of a disused shop on Renshaw Street to the wall of the Liverpool Savings Bank vaults, which contained many thousands of pounds. A small quantity of Atlas Dynamite Powder (procured from a Fenian) was available as another, fall-back option, should the vault walls present too much of an obstacle, but hacking through the stone with picks was preferable to shaking the foundations of Bold Street, and risking a cave-in. The plan was to raid the vaults on Saturday night and to clean them out by Sunday morning. Weekends were always favoured for these types of break-in, for obvious reasons.

Arthur Griffin and his 'butler' – a murderous Mancunian youth who had avoided having to watch the judge don his Black Cap after escaping from detention – heard the distinctive chiselling sounds shortly after nine o'clock that Saturday evening, and realised with dread that some lesser breed of criminal was attempting to rob the bank, which lay almost adjacent to the secret club.

Various plans of action formed in Griffin's mind. He could kill the bank-robbers and then dispose of their bodies – but he would also have to cover up their work, and from the sounds he could hear, the miscreant moles had already tunnelled quite a distance to have come into such proximity of the vault. And what if these amateurs had already attracted the attention of some law-abiding citizen, or alerted some policeman on his beat?

Griffin considered using the crooked copper PC Richard Reeves to survey the tunnel and perhaps frighten the robbers off, but such men would probably be armed, and would be unlikely to relinquish their work with so much prize-money so tantalisingly near. Griffin knew that, come Monday morning, the staff at the Liverpool Savings Bank would report the robbery and soon the police would be crawling all over Bold Street – and Roscoe Street, off which the secret entrance to the club was to be found.

Griffin may have wondered if he and his lackeys should step in and hijack the bank job and snatch the takings from the inferior criminals, but in the end a much more drastic course of action was chosen. He decided that evacuation was the only answer, because he had tasted prison life and detested it. He concluded that it would be downright foolish to risk losing his freedom again.

Fenians bringing in dynamite in cement barrels

He and his henchmen gathered together what they needed and fled from the subterranean club, probably through a tunnel that still runs the length of Renshaw Street – towards the cellars of the Vines public house on the corner of Lime Street and Copperas Hill.

After the flight from danger there were rumours in the criminal underworld which claimed that Griffin had relocated with his criminal clan to a mansion in leafy Aigburth. The budding bank robbers were caught red-handed when a night watchman leaving a pub on the corner of Renshaw and Oldham Streets noticed several suspicious-looking faces peering out from the grimy windows of the vacant shop used by the crooks. Apparently, the manager of the Liverpool Savings Bank tried to suppress any newspaper coverage of the attempted break-in because such news was obviously detrimental to the bank's reputation amongst clients and potential investors.

When detectives routinely surveyed the adjoining buildings to the bank, they came across the deserted private premises on Roscoe Place, and after breaking into the cellar they discovered the door which led to Griffin's former lair. A portable pillar box, used to collect mailed valuables from the unwary, was discovered in one corner, and scattered piles of artificial diamonds of exceptional brilliance were also found strewn about the floor, obviously dropped during the hasty retreat. One policeman found a syringe and a bottle of strong sulphuric acid – used by the more experienced burglar to sizzle through the insides of sophisticated locks via the hypodermic needle. An accidental splash of the opened bottle burnt a hole right through one of the policemen's boots.

Griffin's gang had enjoyed a high level of comfort in their hideaway but had had to leave many of their possessions behind when they made their hasty retreat. The wine cellar had been abandoned, along with the casks of ale and several items of furniture, including an expensive Louis XIV-style sofa, an assortment of chairs and tables and even several beds. A rich aroma of pipe tobacco and the presence of recent newspapers were the only indications of the place being recently inhabited.

By 1894, Arthur Griffin was suffering from a consumptive disease, and was being cared for by Robert and Emily Rickarby of Peel Street, Toxteth Park, his neighbours. At this time Griffin had been living under a false name, but thinking his days were numbered, he confessed his true identity to the Rickarbys, and instructed Robert Rickarby to fetch a large wooden trunk from his home. Griffin was also planning to summon a priest to administer the Last Rites. Robert Rickarby had the suspiciously heavy trunk transported to the bedroom where his friend was apparently dying.

With a great deal of effort Griffin pulled himself up on one elbow and rummaged about underneath his pillow. Shortly he pulled out a large iron key which he handed to his friend.

"Could you please open the box for me, Rickarby? gasped Griffin. "I think you'll be quite surprised at what's inside."

Robert Rickarby opened the box to reveal a veritable treasure horde of gold ingots and coins, as well as breathtaking items of jewellery and bundles of banknotes. He and his wife had never seen such wealth and they exchanged nervous, disapproving glances.

"If I should die, all this is yours. You've been so kind to me," said Griffin, who had sunk back into pillow, exhausted.

The Rickarbys were upright, honest citizens and were genuinely shocked by what they had just seen.

"We cannot accept the ill-gotten loot of a thief," protested Emily, stiffly, and she and Robert left the room in disgust and locked Griffin inside. One of their servants was despatched to summon the police, but when the officers of the law entered Griffin's bedroom, they found the sick-bed still warm, but empty, and a curtain fluttering in front of an open window.

Arthur Griffin had evaded capture wearing nothing but his nightshirt, and despite an intensive manhunt in the area, he was never seen again. The shock of his threatened arrest had obviously restored him to health in the nick of time.

The incredible horde of gold, jewellery and other valuables was removed from 45 Peel Street to Police Headquarters in the city, whilst the upright Rickarbys looked on.

Roscoe Place

The Great Liverpool Scareship

Liverpool Scareship

On the Tuesday night of 28 January 1913, an enormous cigar-shaped airship invaded the airspace over Lancashire. At first its vast bulk was visible only as an ominous silhouette passing noiselessly in front of the star-speckled heavens, and then the 'envelope', or metallic covering of the airship, seemed to light up as it reflected back the streetlights of the city as it passed over Liverpool. Unlike Zeppelins and other airships, the mysterious craft in the sky over Liverpool that night did not have stabilising fins, or a rudder and elevator, nor did it have droning, engine-driven propellers, but it was equipped with a blinding, almost laser-like searchlight, which swept back and forth across great swathes of the city as it glided in from the east.

Early reports of the sinister silent airship came from outside Liverpool, from Warrington, Prescot and St Helens, at around eight o'clock on that frosty Tuesday evening. At around half-past eight, PC John Stott happened to look up and spotted the huge, shadowy sky-ship gliding silently high overhead, as he rode his trusty service bicycle up Carr Lane in West Derby on his way to the

Police Station. He quickly jumped off his bike which he abandoned at the roadside and burst into the Sefton Arms Hotel pub to alert the locals to the presence of the aerial invader. A handful of farmers and local squires rushed outside to see for themselves what the bobby was ranting on about. They too clearly saw the airborne mystery ship coursing through the starry sky in total silence, flashing a powerful searchlight of some kind that created vast, illuminated tracts across farmland and the Church of the Good Shepherd.

The landlord and some of the regulars from the Dog and Gun inn had beheld the same strange spectacle minutes earlier as the airship passed over Ryecroft Farm. Servants, gamekeepers, and the coachman at Croxteth Hall, the nearby ancestral home of the Molyneux family, had also witnessed the eerie flyby of the unidentified airship, and a bewildered old smithy on the outskirts of Norris Green believed that 'Old Nick' himself was paying the region a visit, and scuttled back into his forge and hid behind a pile of scrap iron as the airship ploughed relentlessly on across the night sky.

The airship was next seen hovering over Little Bongs, close to Knotty Ash brewery, where it swept its actinic searchlight back and forth along a section of the Cheshire Lines Railway tracks, before proceeding towards Old Swan. Trams ground to a halt on their icy tracks as the artificial, night-time rays blazed again over Liverpool Cattle Market and Green Lane Waterworks. By the time the airship was over Edge Hill, terrifying rumours were flying about concerning the menacing aerial trespasser.

At a pub called the Boundary, situated on the corner of Lodge Lane and Smithdown Road, an irresponsible old veteran of the Boer War named Carter claimed that the airship hanging over the neighbourhood was actually a German Zeppelin, carrying out surveillance work in preparation for a bombing raid on the Town Hall and the docks. Carter assured all his fellow drinkers that he had it "on good authority" from a military man (actually a drunken night watchman on Penny Lane) that Britain would be at war with Germany from midnight that night. When the drinkers rushed out of the saloon bar, they could see what they were convinced was the Kaiser's dreadnought of the sky, training its superior searchlight on the marshalling grid irons and Edge Hill railway station. Confirmation enough for Carter's assertions. Carter's rumour of imminent war continued to spread through the maze of terraced streets, triggering localised hysteria for the remainder of that night.

The airship, meanwhile, was being steered relentlessly towards the airspace over the city by its unknown pilot. The newly-built Adelphi Hotel came under the heavenly spotlight, as did the old Lewis's store. The intense beam of light also briefly lit up St George's Hall and Lime Street Station, and when the 'Zeppelin' then began to move at an incredible speed of around twenty-five miles per hour towards the docks, the awestruck public followed its path, full of foreboding.

Finally, the airship's unidentified aeronauts brought their craft to a standstill directly above Canning Dock. From that vantage point, the ghostly light beam then began to scan the Albert, Salthouse and King's docks.

By this time, the rumours of an impending war had firmly taken hold, and the airship was regarded by many as nothing less than the first of an airborne vanguard crossing the North Sea from Germany with the conquest of Britain in its sights. An aerial invasion had been viewed as a possibility for some time, ever since, four years earlier, in 1909, pioneering aviator Louis Bleriot became the first pilot to cross the English Channel in a monoplane, in an historic thirty-seven-minute flight. He picked up one thousand pounds in prize money from Lord Northcliffe, the man who had challenged pilots to become the first to cross the Channel by powered flight. Northcliffe, the owner of the Daily Mail newspaper, promptly announced, in dramatic, front-page headlines in his newspaper, that: 'England is no longer an island'. It was soon realised that the end of our isolation from the continent was a two-edged sword. The protective moat around this sceptred isle had been rendered useless by the new flying machines, making us much more vulnerable to attack from an alien power, and now Britain's naval supremacy seemed suddenly redundant. Furthermore, there were worrying rumours that Bleriot had not actually been the first person to cross the Channel after all ...

In the Spring of 1909, some months before Bleriot's historic flight, there had been many alleged sightings of unmarked airships crossing the Channel and the North Sea from the continent, and most people seemed to think that the invaders were German Zeppelins. These airships travelled at much greater speeds than any airship in existence and also carried extremely powerful searchlights. The Press ridiculed the so-called 'scareships', as they nicknamed them, but the first Zeppelin raids on East Anglia finally did become a reality six years later in 1917.

In 1908, five years before the mysterious airship visited Lancashire, newspapers in London serialised HG Well's novel 'The War in the Air', which described airships destroying New York with high-explosive bombs. So, when many freethinking and well-read Liverpudlians saw the unidentified airship over their city, they jumped to the conclusion that it marked the prelude to a German invasion.

Fortunately, on that chilly Tuesday night, the airship, having hung over Canning Dock for some time, abruptly turned off its light and sped away to the north at a speed which no known Zeppelin could attain. It vanished back into the darkness from which it came, and the incident was quickly forgotten.

Was the airship some foreign power's prototype dirigible, or were its origins much more sinister? Many UFOs seen in the 1950s and 1960s were also cigar-shaped, so some ufologists have hypothesised that the torpedo-shaped craft seen in the early twentieth century were extra-terrestrial in origin. The riddle of the unidentified airship remains unsolved, but we may discover more about it one day.

The Fate of Captain Black

Captain Black

Many years ago, in the late 1980s, I set off on one of my first-ever 'ghost hunts' with a group of like-minded people whose ages ranged from late teens to late fifties. I suggested calling our recently-formed group The Forteans – as we were investigating what were known as Fortean phenomena (named after the great Charles Fort, who catalogued a succession of strange reports unearthed in his delvings in the libraries of London and New York). I don't think my suggestion was taken up, and someone put forward an immediately forgettable acronym instead.

Anyway, around six or seven of us were allowed into the area around the old disused airfields of what was then Speke Airport, in search of an apparition – alleged to be that of a pilot from the early days of flying – which had been sighted near a runway. On that morning, the North West was blinded by a blanket of thick fog, which had dramatically reduced visibility. Graham, a retired teacher from Hunts Cross, didn't mind the obscuring fog, as it gave him the opportunity to use the expensive, infra-red camera which he always had at the ready for just such a day as this. The camera could peer through mists which were impenetrable to the human eye.

Ghost hunting is a very slow and tedious business, requiring enormous patience, and none of us was really surprised when we saw absolutely nothing unusual that morning. At around noon we stopped for a break and, despite the inclement weather, were enjoying a picnic close to the runway. The conversation revolved around the frustrations of the morning and the general conclusion was that we were probably going to be equally disappointed by the end of the afternoon.

Then, at around one o'clock, one of our group, a girl named Sheena, leapt to her feet. She said that she'd spotted the shadowy figure of a man walking through the fog in the distance. She quickly picked up a pair of binoculars which had yellow fog filters fitted to the lenses and soon located and then focused on her target. She described what she was looking at to the rest of the group; the man wore a one-piece suit, and had dark, slicked-back hair and an old-fashioned, pencil moustache.

I quickly ventured into the depths of the fog, closely followed by a man named Jim, who was spending a two-week holiday from his mundane job working for an electricity company delving into the murky world of the paranormal. I thought I saw the outline of a man walking unnaturally quickly away from Jim and myself, and, using a walkie-talkie from Tandy, I radioed the details of the visual sighting to Graham, who was only a matter of a few hundred yards away, scanning us and the possible ghost with his infra-red camera. Two other men were taking readings of the earth's magnetic field using an expensive magnetometer, listening in the ultrasonic range, and Sheena had an old tripod-mounted SLR camera, trained in our direction, but it would be of little use with so much fog about.

"I have a target," crackled the voice of Graham in my walkie-talkie and then he explained that he had detected three moving spots of body heat with the infra-red camera. The heat from me and Jim – and the elusive, unidentified man with the pencil moustache. "He's moving to the north now, he's quite close," Graham told us via the radio transceiver, yet we could no longer see anyone.

Then came the chilling words from the ex-teacher, "He's actually just passed through the two of you!"

We had felt nothing; no cold shiver running through our bodies, such as other witnesses have reported when ghosts have walked through them.

The investigation came to no firm conclusion, only that a ghost was definitely at large on that airfield, and that he had been seen by several people working at Speke Airport over a period of many years. The mysterious phantom's nickname was 'Captain Black', but no one seemed to know how, or why, such an unusual name had been assigned to him .

The few people I knew who hunted ghosts at that time always smirked at the mere mention of Captain Black, and made scathing remarks about the Captain Scarlet character often seen on television in the 1960s and 1970s. I resolved to beat the sceptics at their own game and satisfy my own curiosity at the same time by trying to discover if such a captain really did exist – the name must have come from somewhere, I argued.

So it was that I began to trawl through the local newspaper archives searching for clues. I was certainly surprised by the information I uncovered. It was relatively simple to establish the fact that Captain Thomas Campbell Black had been a dashing, debonair pilot of the 1930s, who had won the London to Melbourne Air Race in 1934 in a DH Comet in the record-breaking time of two days, twenty-two hours, and fifty-four minutes. But what had become of him after the race, I wondered, and I set about digging even deeper into the archives.

In September 1936, Captain Black was invited to the Adelphi Hotel in Liverpool to be the guest of honour at a special dinner given by Mr John Moores, the famous local businessman and entrepreneur. The highlight of the evening came when Mr Moores presented a three thousand pound aeroplane – Miss Liverpool I – to the people of Liverpool, and it was to be piloted by Captain Black on the following day in an aerial race from Portsmouth to Johannesburg.

I came across a photograph of the legendary Captain Thomas Campbell Black among the various newspaper archives – and it showed him to be a very striking individual, with dark, slicked-back hair and a pencil moustache – just like the man we had spotted at the airport. Intrigued, I read on about Black. He had been interviewed by a local reporter from the Evening Standard who had asked him several questions about the forthcoming race to Johannesburg, and what it meant to him. Black had remarked: "I really do not know why I am making this Johannesburg trip. I think it's because the thrill of a race always appeals to me. I feel I stand a very good chance of winning the race – if everything goes all right. The plane is everything that she was expected to be and I believe that she will be able to get up to a speed of two hundred and seventy miles an hour."

The reporter mentioned the possibility of something going dangerously wrong on the non-stop flight, to which Black replied, enigmatically: "Personally, I think the odds in the way of danger are slightly higher against the pilot taking part in an air race."

Captain Black was generous in his praise of the aeroplane which John Moores had presented to the city of Liverpool: "There is one thing that has largely influenced me in deciding to make this flight. That is that I am convinced that I will have the finest ship for the job it is possible to obtain. I am confident that she can make the trip faster than any other craft I may be up against, but of course, so much depends on conditions and that little, but very important, thing we call luck. With ordinary luck I will win. If the luck is against me ..." and here Captain Black gave a little half smile, then added, "... I'll keep on flying to the end."

Later that evening at the Adelphi Hotel ballroom, Captain Black presented a small silver model of the plane, Miss Liverpool I, to John Moores, who thanked him for the reciprocal gesture and wished him luck in the race.

On the following day – Saturday 19 September 1936 – Captain Thomas Campbell Black climbed into the cockpit of Miss Liverpool I at Speke Airport, bound for London, from where he would fly to Portsmouth to start the race. Crowds of well-wishers and curious sight-seers had gathered to wave him off on yet another epic flight. The majority of them looked on from three hundred feet away, but a handful of people had managed to get close enough to the runway to be able to see the pilot through the cockpit window.

One of these nearby witnesses was Mabel Chorlton, a widow from Garston. Mrs Chorlton prided herself on having perfect vision, and from where she was standing she could plainly see that Captain Black was holding what appeared to be a piece of foolscap paper in his right hand. She noted that he had his head bowed, and was avidly reading from the piece of paper, even as the plane moved out of its enclosure. The pilot's eyes were glued to whatever was written, or printed, on that piece of paper, and he was so engrossed that he failed to notice the RAF Hawker Hart light bomber which was coming in to land. The plane was heading directly towards Miss Liverpool I – on a straight collision course.

The crowd of spectators realised what was happening and gasped in horror. Captain Andrews, manager of Speke Airport, assumed that Black had seen the bomber coming in to land on the runway – but the pilot of Miss Liverpool I was still too distracted by the piece of paper he was reading. Flying Officer Peter Stanley Salter, of 611 County of Lancaster Bombing Squadron, was flying the RAF bomber solo on a test run. He had made a circuit over Speke Aerodrome, then flown down the Mersey before making a left turn which manoeuvred him into the correct position for a smooth gliding descent down to the runway at Speke Airport.

As the bomber slowed in its descent, its nose went up slightly, creating a blind area where the pilot could not see the ground straight ahead of him. Salter had seen Miss Liverpool I in the enclosure as he glided down towards the runway, but had no idea that Captain Black was now in the path of the taxi-ing bomber as it rolled along the runway. Screams from the spectators rent the air as they realised that a terrible tragedy was about to unfold, right in front of their eyes. Captain Black's attention was still fully concentrated upon the sheet of paper that he was holding in his right hand as the bomber ploughed into his plane. He stood no chance; he sustained appalling injuries in the impact and died from lacerated lungs, haemorrhage and shock. Amazingly, the pilot of the RAF bomber escaped from the accident unscathed.

Meanwhile, in London, Captain Black's actress wife, Florence Desmond, was busy rehearsing for a play at the Victoria Palace theatre, when the tragic news was broken to her. Her reaction to being told of her husband's untimely death was rather strange and unemotional to say the least. She said that she felt quite numbed by the news, but insisted that the show would go on at the theatre that night, come what may: "I am just going to go on with my job, as Tom would have wanted me to do," she said.

Florence Desmond was spared the trauma of being called upon to identify her husband's body when the late captain's father, H Milner Black, the ex-Mayor of Brighton, made the journey to Liverpool to formally identify his son.

What could possibly have been written upon that mysterious sheet of foolscap paper which was so utterly riveting, that it cost Captain Thomas Campbell Black his life? No one knows the answer to that conundrum, for it seems that the mysterious piece of paper could not be found anywhere amongst the plane's wreckage. It must have contained something truly shocking to make such a highly trained pilot forget all the safety drills he had been taught and be totally oblivious to the movements of another aeroplane coming in to land. Could it possibly have been a 'Dear John' letter from the captain's stage-struck wife? Was Florence Desmond's reaction to the news of Captain Black's death normal for someone who was in love with her husband? Even the most dedicated actor or actress would find it well nigh impossible to perform on stage after receiving such a shocking piece of news, yet this is exactly what she did. However, this is all pure speculation and we may never know the real reason for Captain Black's uncharacteristic behaviour on that fateful day.

A short while after the tragedy, the first sightings of Captain Black's ghost were reported in the vicinity of some hangars which overlooked the scene of the fatal crash. The anguished expression on the ghost's face is something that is frequently mentioned by witnesses, and so we can assume that the long-dead airman is not at rest because of some unfinished business which keeps his spirit earthbound.

It is said that the ghost of Captain Black still continues to haunt the peripheries of what has now become John Lennon Airport.

The King of Arguments

Jonathan Flynn

In the late 1880s, an extraordinary incident, said to be of a supernatural nature, allegedly took place in the centre of Liverpool. The setting for this peculiar tale was the Dewdrop Inn, on the corner of Wood Street and Hanover Street. The pub was later renamed the Empire, and it still stands today.

Around 1889, the so-called 'King of Arguments' was at large in Liverpool; a man exceptionally skilled in the art of rhetoric – or the 'gift of the gab', as Liverpudlians would say. Flynn could win any argument, against all-comers, and thrived on making outlandish claims and then defending them using his amazing verbal acuity.

His name (he maintained) was Jonathan Flynn, and he was obviously a man of considerable private means, as he never seemed to do any work, but nevertheless managed to dress elegantly in very expensive suits and wore nothing but the finest silk top hats and cravats. His favourite tipple was absinthe and he always smoked luxurious French cigarettes, so naturally he stood out from the crowd when he made one of his frequent evening visits to the Dewdrop Inn. He lived in the lap of luxury in his palatial residence in the desirable suburb of St Michael's in the Hamlet, a couple of miles outside the city centre.

One rainy summer's evening, Flynn was about to enter his favourite watering hole, the Dewdrop Inn, when he found his way barred by two ragged children, a boy and a girl, both aged about eight years of age, although small for their age like so many malnourished street children in the city. The boy, whose pinched face was in desperate need of a wash and whose filthy hair was a tangled mop, asked Flynn for a few pennies, explaining that his twin sister was blind and that they were both orphans. Flynn's reaction to the boy's request was typical of the man's arrogance.

"The poor will always be with us. The Bible said that. Why should I give you money?" he said, looking down at the barefoot children with ill-concealed contempt.

Initially, the boy was stuck for words, but he decided to have one last try.

"But, sir, me and me sister Nelly is so 'ungry. Please spare us a few pennies, just a few pennies, sir."

"A few pennies! A few pennies! I'd be bankrupt if I gave a few pennies to every ragamuffin I met." Flynn ranted. "It's an absolute outrage – a gentleman cannot walk the streets of this accursed city without being accosted by some filthy beggar or another. Be off with you both before I call ..."

A sudden downpour cut short Flynn's sermon and he rushed into the saloon of the Dewdrop Inn to avoid getting drenched, leaving the two pathetic children huddled together in the doorway. He found just three drinkers propping up the bar in the parlour, but he knew each of them well. They were in the middle of a conversation about the mysteries of the human brain. Flynn always became impatient when he was not the centre of attention, or had not initiated the topic of conversation and he soon interrupted the three men with a seemingly wild tale.

"When I saw action in the second Afghan War, I was in position behind a stone wall in Kabul, right in the thick of it, when Sergeant Jolly Phillips, who was standing next to me, unwisely removed his helmet because of the heat. At that moment a volley of shots rang out and next thing, the top of his head was gone." The drinkers gasped at the brutal spectacle he had conjured up in their minds, and Flynn, enjoying the reaction he had provoked in his audience, continued. "Jolly lifted his hand up to feel where the top of his head had been, and instead felt nothing but space and then the bloody stump of his severed neck. Then he said to me, 'I feel queer, Flynn.' For some reason he started whistling, then closed his eyes and died."

"Impossible!" said one drinker.

"Absolute Poppycock!" agreed another.

"You expect us to believe that!" laughed a third. "You must think we're a bunch of imbeciles!"

But his detractors were soon silenced when Flynn, thoroughly enjoying the moment, reached into the pocket of his tailcoat and, with a theatrical flourish, carefully unfolded a yellowed cutting from an 1879 edition of The Times newspaper. The cutting detailed the freak and tragic death of a Sergeant Jolly Phillips, exactly as Flynn had described it. The three drinkers could see that the article was genuine and reluctantly had to apologise. It wasn't the first time they had challenged the truth of one of Flynn's tales, only to be presented with absolute proof by the infuriating raconteur.

Later that night, the concept of perpetual motion came up for discussion, and everyone present agreed that it was impossible, except, of course, for Flynn. He claimed that a pendulum swinging on a magnetically suspended axis, inside a vacuum jar, would go on swinging to and fro forever, for there would be no air friction to slow it down. "It would, in effect, be a perpetual motion motor," Flynn explained to the lesser mortals who had gathered round him in the bar.

A Mr Balem, a rich merchant, and manager of the Liverpool Art Club, became involved in the debate, and confidently stated that perpetual motion was a scientific impossibility, and that any so-called perpetual motor would inevitably run down in the end, as nothing could rotate under its own power for even so long as an hour. Balem was a prominent and well-respected local figure and the assembled drinkers nodded in agreement. But Balem had played right into Jonathan Flynn's hands and he bet him the sum of one hundred pounds that he could demonstrate such perpetual motion within the next five minutes. Eyebrows were raised but the arguers shook hands on it, and Balem turned to a friend and quipped, "This will be the easiest one hundred guineas I have ever made!"

Flynn took Balem by the arm and escorted him outside. He pointed up at the stars and patiently explained: "The stars rise and set because the earth is constantly spinning, and this has gone on since the beginning of time, and will continue for eternity. The earth's rotation is the perfect example of perpetual motion."

An embarrassed "Hmph!" was all that the humiliated Balem could manage and he stormed off up Hanover Street.

A gaggle of drinkers who had watched the whole drama unfold chortled to themselves, knowing that once again, 'Slippery Flynn' had proved himself right. It is not known whether Mr Balem paid up, but the drinking, the tall stories and the arguing went on for the remainder of that night.

At one point during the evening, the absinthe-sodden Flynn settled himself into a comfortable seat in the parlour and dozed off for a short time. He quickly sank into a most peculiar and sharply realistic dream. In this dream, Flynn was leaving the Dewdrop Inn, and a full moon loomed low over the city, painting everything silver. He lit a cigarette and was strolling along Hanover Street when a strange, black, four-wheeled 'growler' coach creaked to a halt alongside him. The coachman was just a black silhouette perched on his seat in the front of the vehicle, and from inside the coach, a mellifluous and slightly mocking voice called out, "My word! It's the famous Mr Flynn!"

The door of the growler opened and a distinguished-looking gentleman with a moon-white face beckoned him into the coach. Flynn found himself drawn to wards the vehicle, in an almost hypnotic trance. The coachman clambered down from his seat and respectfully pulled down the folding steps and held open the door. Flynn stepped inside the coach and noted that the eminent-looking man was of a rather Mephistophelean appearance, with his Vandyke beard, curled up moustache, dark penetrating eyes, and decidedly pointed ears. He wore a suit of vivid, grass-green velvet and smoked a noxious pipe which caused a choking, sulphurous atmosphere to build up inside the coach as soon as the door was closed. The stranger introduced himself as the Devil, in a matter-of-fact way, and informed Jonathan Flynn that he was taking him to straight to Hell.

Flynn immediately tried to prise open the door of the coach but it seemed to be welded shut. The evil-looking man who professed to be the Devil incarnate giggled, and said, "If you can win an argument with the Devil, I may consider letting you go."

The coach trundled off and soon picked up speed, but instead of the sensation of forward motion which Flynn was expecting, the coach seemed to be travelling steeply downwards. So rapid was the descent that Flynn had to grip the armrests and his stomach churned. After some time, an unearthly scarlet light started to filter into the dark interior of the growler. By this time the atmosphere inside the carriage was so thick with acrid smoke that Flynn was finding it difficult to breathe. He began to choke and cough and begged the Devil to extinguish his pipe. Surprisingly, the menacing man in green did as Flynn implored, and then challenged his victim to try and trick him with his legendary argumentative skills. Normally Flynn would have risen to such a challenge with relish but on this occasion he was so afraid that he couldn't think straight and could only mumble something unintelligible by way of reply.

The coach then screeched to an abrupt halt, and lurched crazily backwards and forwards on its suspension. As it did so, the dreadful sounds of distant screaming and moaning could be heard – sounds which conjured up images of tortured souls burning in everlasting fire and which chilled Jonathan Flynn to the bone. He shuddered, trying to imagine what terrible fate the Devil had in store for him. He sank to his knees in the cramped coach and begged to be taken back to earth, away from what were obviously the outer reaches of Hell.

"You're asleep, you do know that, don't you?" said the Devil to his quarry. Flynn was puzzled but felt no sense of relief. "Yes, this is a dream, but I can easily prevent you from waking … ever …" said the Evil One with glee.

"Please take me back! Please! I'll do anything!" begged Flynn, trembling violently as the sounds of wailing increased in intensity and the carriage grew uncomfortably hot as the red glow turned the inside of the coach into a fiery furnace.

"Give me one good reason why I should spare your wretched life!" said the Devil, his voice suddenly deafening. He was now incandescent with rage, and leaned over the kneeling, quivering man. "I am very old and I am very wise," hissed Satan. "And I can twist the truth and win any argument, so give me one good reason why I should let you wake up!"

Flynn struggled to muster his usual rhetorical skills and to employ his usual tricks which had helped him to triumph in so many arguments in the past. But they now deserted him entirely and he couldn't concentrate because he was so terrified. Then, suddenly, like a ray of light in the darkness of his desperate mind, Flynn saw, in his mind's eye, an image of the little ragged-clothed boy and his blind sister outside the Dewdrop Inn.

"Nelly!" Flynn answered at last.

"The blind girl?" the Devil asked, as if he were capable of reading Flynn's mind.

"Yes," said Flynn, "I want to live so that I can help her and her brother and others like her."

The Devil let out a truly blood-curdling scream, which made Flynn screw up his eyes and put his hands over his ears. The horrible sound was still ringing in his ears when he woke up in the parlour of the Dewdrop Inn, gasping for breath and sweating profusely. As his eyes began to focus he slowly realised where he was and that a policeman and the pub landlord were anxiously leaning over him. The publican was clutching a bottle of smelling salts in his hand and was passing it to and fro beneath Flynn's nose and the policeman was shaking him by the shoulder and calling out his name.

"Mr Flynn! Wake up, sir. Mr Flynn … Jonathan!"

"Bless my soul, he's alive!" exclaimed the landlord. "My word! We thought you were a goner then, sir."

The two men struggled to help Flynn to his feet, obviously greatly relieved that they were not having to deal with a dead body. Having decided that Flynn had suffered some kind of unconsciousness or fit, the policeman walked the King of Arguments about outside in the cool night air of Wood Street until he became steady on his feet. Eventually, Flynn, although he still felt groggy, assured the policeman that he was able to take care of himself. And so, after watching him for a while, the constable saluted Flynn and resumed his beat.

Jonathan Flynn thought long and hard about the frighteningly realistic nightmare he had experienced in the pub, and wondered if it was purely the product of his over-indulgence with absinthe – a notoriously toxic drink – or had it some deeper significance? He had had nightmares before after drinking absinthe, but never like this one, and he felt somehow chastened by the experience.

As he walked along moonlit Hanover Street, still feeling decidedly woosey, the familiar, black, four-wheeled growler coach rolled up alongside him once again. With an impending sense of déjà vu, Flynn started to recall the details of the horrifying dream of the Devil in the growler. It all came back to him with alarming clarity – he could even smell the sulphurous, choking fumes from the Devil's filthy pipe. His heart began to race and he quickened his pace, turning up Bold Street to avoid the diabolical coach. All he wanted to do was to get back to the security of his home in St Michael's in the Hamlet as quickly as possible, and he began to scan the street for a hansom cab which could take him there.

During his search for a hansom cab, Flynn came upon little blind Nelly and her brother shivering in the doorway of one of the shops up Bold Street. The rain had now stopped but the pair were still wet through from the earlier downpour and they had nothing but their rags with which to keep themselves warm. He was filled with shame when he recalled his behaviour towards the destitute children – helpless, fellow human beings – earlier in the evening, and he now saw, with absolute clarity, just how callous he had been. He also recalled his vivid dream and what he had promised the Devil at the gates of Hell. Apparently, he decided that from that night onwards, he would take the two urchins under his wing.

All Flynn's arrogance seemed to evaporate as a result of that life-changing dream and he no longer spent his evenings frequenting the saloons of Liverpool. The terrifyingly realistic dream, in which he was convinced that he had had an encounter with the Devil, transformed his character and from that day on, he became a teetotal champion of the city's poor.

Dewdrop Inn

Strange Mirages

Mirage of a city seen over Liverpool

No book on strange local incidents would be complete without an account of the wide-scale sightings of a 'city' seen in the skies over Liverpool on several occasions during the Victorian period. At the time of the sightings, the witnesses to the gigantic distant city floating above the clouds were adamant that what they had seen was a real, solid metropolis, which had somehow freed itself from the gravity which makes us all prisoners of the earth.

So-called experts who had never set eyes upon the aerial city tried to explain away the sightings as nothing more than the product of a mirage – a refracted, or reflected, image of some actual distant city, projected on to clouds and mist as a result of varying temperatures in the atmosphere. However, several amateur astronomers who scrutinised the Laputa-like flying city over Liverpool were in agreement with the other witnesses; they could plainly see that, rather than some ghostly image of a terrestrial town projected on to cloud, what they were looking at was actually a bizarre-looking, three-dimensional, circular island, upon which were built intricate conurbations made up of domes, towers and pyramidal structures.

Various estimates in terms of size were ascribed to the city in the sky by an assortment of both professional and casual observers; these varied widely, ranging from one mile in diameter to almost ten miles in circumference.

At the centre of the disc-shaped city there towered a vast pyramid-shaped structure which was clearly visible to anyone with access to a telescope. An astronomer at Birkenhead Park claimed that he could clearly distinguish the pyramid, whereas naked-eye observers interpreted the structure as a geographical feature, some kind of enormous central mountain, or land mass, rising up between the buildings.

The alarming apparition of the city in the heavens was first noticed at 2.55pm on the Sunday afternoon of 27 September 1846, by a watchman who was guarding the building site of the New Philharmonic Hall on Hope Street. Mr Morris was sipping tea laced with rum as he sat inside his railed enclosure. It was a chilly day and the rum helped to keep out the cold, even though he knew it was strictly forbidden to drink whilst on duty. Morris warmed his hands by cupping them round the mug, whilst the hot liquid warmed his insides. Something suddenly made him look up and it was then that he noticed something enormous emerging from a cloud and passing into another one high above the Liverpool Workhouse. The watchman noticed that the fleeting object was following a west-to-east trajectory.

A lapsed Presbyterian, Mr Morris immediately interpreted the spectacle as being some kind of warning vision from God, perhaps admonishing him because he was drinking liquor on the Sabbath – whilst on duty, to boot. As soon as his shift was over, he made a hurried visit to the Presbyterian church on Canning Street to speak to a minister – he needed to get the whole matter off his chest. He confessed his sin and told the minister all about the 'omen' he had seen in the sky.

Meanwhile, as Mr Morris was gulping down his mug of rum-spiked tea, full of fear and apprehension, the city in the sky was drifting steadily in a straight line over Kirkdale, where it understandably caused a great deal of consternation amongst the ordinary, and largely uneducated, folk of that borough. An Irish Catholic priest walking up Richmond Hill bore witness to the disc-like mass of unfamiliar structures gliding overhead between the low cloud cover, and later confided to a fellow priest that he had at first wondered if he was seeing the holy city which St John had beheld coming down from heaven over Patmos in the Bible's Book of Revelation. However, the priest soon came to the conclusion that there was something spectral and much more sinister about the airborne city. It was constantly metamorphosing as it journeyed across the heavens; seeming to fluctuate and scintillate, transforming itself into some insubstantial fortress made of nothing more than rainbows and aurorae as it passed directly overhead.

The priest recalled the tales he'd heard during his childhood back in Ireland about the 'Duna Feadhreagh – enchanted fairy castles in the air that had been seen floating over the coasts of Antrim, Donegal and Waterford. A Celtic colleague of the priest, a Scot of seventy years of age named MacDonald, who was engaged in the brick-by-brick removal of Rupert's Hut at the time, agreed that the levitating city roving through the atmosphere above them was but a figment of the 'Brownies' – the little supernatural folk he had met as a child on the Isle of Arran. MacDonald had himself been witness to a very similar, awe-inspiring sight at the age of six. Out at sea, to the west of Arran, high over the Mull of Kintyre, a far-off floating island, crowned with a golden city's shimmering skyline, often appeared in the clouds, featuring street after street of gleaming houses, the turrets of gigantic castles, tall towers and smoking chimneys. Sometimes the sharp-sighted were even able to discern the citizens of this fabulous sky-city, dressed in strangely-coloured clothing, running to and fro on the streets.

Naturally, there were endless interpretations and attempts to explain the appearance of the enigmatic city in the sky, which was seen for a duration of forty minutes before it vanished back into the clouds as mysteriously as it had first arrived. The theories ranged from the feasible, to the downright bizarre. One of the strangest came from within the scientific community – a group of astronomers and meteorologists blamed unusual weather conditions for producing an illusory image of the city of Edinburgh in the sky over Liverpool! Edinburgh is three hundred and twenty-five kilometres north east of Liverpool, but as mirages go, this distance pales into insignificance when we ponder the following mirage reports.

When the first white settlers reached Alaska, the Native Indians they found there spoke of the ghostly image of a village in the sky that appeared regularly in the summer.

In 1887 this legendary village appeared in the Alaskan skies over Mount

Fairweather, and was actually captured with a camera by a man named Willoughby. Some investigators claimed that the phantom city of Alaska was a in fact a mirage of Bristol, of all places, thousands of miles away in England, whereas others hypothesised that the apparition was more likely to be some ghostly flashback of a city that once existed in Alaska's distant past.

Sixty-seven years previously, a Captain Scoresby, master of the ship Baffin, had beheld a similarly perplexing sight when he was gazing through his telescope at the then unexplored coastline of Greenland, looking for natural harbours, or suitable places to weigh anchor. To his astonishment, he beheld, 'An extensive ancient city abounding with the ruins of castle, obelisks, churches and monuments, with other large and inconspicuous buildings.'

No satisfactory explanation for these sightings has ever been put forward.

There have been countless other reports of spectral cities in the skies all over the world, from Ohio in North America, to Ghelma in North Africa.

In the 1880s, another city in the sky was said to have been sighted over Lancashire, but the precise date of the incident is unknown. In 2002, a Mike Walker sent me a copy of an intriguing photograph which he had found amongst a bundle of Victorian ephemera that he had purchased in Quiggins, in Liverpool city centre. The photograph shows an extensive, ghost-like castle suspended in the sky over an unidentified city. An undated caption on the back, written in faded ink, reads, 'Mirage over Lancashire'.

Nothing more is known about the subject matter of the remarkable photograph, and we still remain in the dark concerning the 1846 city in the sky incident.

The Case of the Greek Vampire

40 Upper Parliament Street

In Victorian times the merchants who grew rich in the bustling port of Liverpool wanted mansions which befitted their status and announced to the world that they were people of consequence. In the late 1860s, one such merchant, Nathaniel Cain, who had grown wealthy through his dealings in iron ore, bought himself a magnificent mansion at 40 Upper Parliament Street, and hired a cortège of servants to wait upon him. Cain was a lover of fine wine, and decided to extend the cellars beneath his new property to accommodate his extensive collection of expensive Clarets, Chardonnays and Champagnes.

Workmen were brought in to remodel and extend the existing cellar, and in the course of their excavations, they came upon what appeared to be a tomb of polished granite. Upon one of the walls of this tomb was a Christian cross, and a plaque inscribed with obscure glyphs which resembled letters of the Greek alphabet.

Georgio Eustratiadi, a merchant of Italian origin and a close friend of Nathaniel Cain, was invited into the cellar to take a look at the 'tomb' and give his opinion as to what course of action to take. Eustratiadi did not spend long in the cellar and as soon as he came out he advised his associate not to enter the cubic vault, whose sides all measured about nine feet. It was obvious that something had unnerved the Italian, who nervously made the sign of the cross as he told his bemused friend that he had experienced a strong sensation that something evil and threatening lay within the burial vault. Mr Cain laughed and told him that he was just being superstitious, it was an ordinary tomb and nothing more. It was just in an unusual place, that was all. He said that he would report the vault to the authorities, so that if it did contain any mortal remains, they could be re-interred in a proper churchyard.

The authorities were not informed, however, and a group of privately-hired workmen set about excavating around the strange vault. One of the workmen suggested that it might be better to leave the stone structure intact, as it would help support the roof of the extended wine cellar. Cain however, had a burning, morbid curiosity to discover just who, or what, lay within that vault, and he agonised about what course of action to take. Deep down he felt that it would be an act of desecration to look into the tomb, but his intense inquisitiveness overrode any moral considerations.

Some weeks after the discovery of the enigmatic tomb, the servants at Cain's house claimed that they had started to hear strange sounds coming from the wine cellar. Again, Cain simply dismissed their claims as pure superstition, although, by now, he too was beginning to feel that the tomb had something creepy about it.

Then, three days after the workmen had completed their remodelling of the cellar, Nathaniel Cain himself heard the eerie sound of a man singing in the early hours of the morning, and the sound filled him with dread. From that point on he felt ill at ease in the house which should have been his pride and joy. On one occasion, as a bitter wind from the Mersey howled along Upper Parliament Street, Nathaniel Cain arose from his bed at four in the morning, clutching a pistol in one hand and a lit candle in the other. With his heart thumping he descended the stairs, and heard not only the strains of someone singing in a foreign language, but also the eerie sounds of the singer's manic, shrieking laughter, which seemed to reverberate around the hall as if it were mocking him. With a shudder, Cain realised that the origin of the uncanny nocturnal racket was the spooky cellar and, rather than investigate further, he decided to turn around and leave the hallway to go back to the safety of his bedroom.

A solicitor from nearby Montpellier Terrace named Thomas Paget had studied Ancient Greek at university, and Mr Cain invited him into the wine cellar with a view to, hopefully, decoding the baffling inscription on the vault and so throw some light on the mysterious goings on. After Paget had read the inscription by the light of a lantern, he unashamedly scurried back up the cellar steps, followed closely by the iron merchant Cain, who was naturally curious as to what had so unnerved his colleague. Paget, clearly shaken, told him that the writing had been barely legible but that he he had been able to read some parts – enough to get the gist of the inscription. Apparently, it was a warning that the soul of the person within the vault was so downright wicked that it could not be allowed within the realms of the dead. A word unknown to Paget – 'vurculac' – was referred to twice in the engraved message and he had made a note of it. He lost no time in consulting one of the books in his father's library and discovered, to his horror, that vurculac – according to ancient East European folklore – was a type of vampire.

Nathaniel Cain and Thomas Paget then began to research the history of 40 Upper Parliament Street, and found that no church had ever stood on the site, so the vault could not have belonged to some forgotten graveyard of yore. By this time neither Cain nor his servants could rest in their beds at night, so worried were they by the strange nocturnal sounds in the house. Nathaniel Cain knew that he had to do something to restore harmony to the house and, according to Georgio Eustratiadi, he paid a sect of monks a huge sum of money to dismantle the vault and dispose of it, along with its contents. They told the coal merchant that all the tomb contained was a yellowed burial shroud, whose ancient material disintegrated immediately upon contact with the air. The monks blessed the wine cellar, and told Cain that a vampiric being which had lain in the tomb until it had been disturbed, had probably gone to ground in a nearby cemetery.

Strangely enough, about a month later, one of the elderly servants at Cain's mansion informed her master that she had answered the door one evening to find a man dressed in a black cape standing on the doorstep. The man had said absolutely nothing when she wished him good evening, but had simply stared at her with dark menacing eyes; "Smiling like the Devil himself," said the servant who had had to be given a large brandy to calm her frayed nerves after the encounter. After standing there in silence for some time, the weird looking visitor had uttered something unintelligible and then lurched forward, but the startled maid managed to slam the door on him. Although it was obvious that the maid was distressed, Cain dismissed her claim as the product of her Irish imagination. However, the master of the household later heard of other reports of the eerie man in black from the most unlikely source.

In January 1870, the Greek Orthodox Church of St Nicholas was consecrated on Liverpool's Berkley Street – just around the corner from Cain's mansion. A religious friend of Cain named John Stanley had actually met the Most Reverend Alexander Lycurgus, the Archbishop of Syra and Tenos, who had consecrated the newly-built Greek Church. After the consecration ceremony, an Anglican minister and a Greek priest talked about a strange-looking man who had been caught trying to steal the chalice containing the Holy Eucharist from the Greek Church. Moreover, this man wore a black, wide-brimmed hat, a cape, and had a sinister, pallid face from which a pair of intensely staring eyes peered out. He had dashed off from the church, leaving his would-be captor clutching his cape, and then run away with amazing speed into the evening gloom, in the direction of Catherine Street.

Archbishop Lycurgus and the Greek priest were united in their opinion that the individual who had attempted to steal the Eucharist was a 'Vyrolakos' – a type of vampire found in countries off the Adriatic and Aegean coasts. Some of the Anglican ministers tried to defuse the spine-chilling talk of vampires by bringing the conversation back to more mundane matters, but Mr Stanley was intrigued and asked the Greek priest what the so-called vampire could possibly want with the Eucharist. "Perhaps to desecrate the most powerful and important part of the Mass in a ritual of black magic," the Greek minister answered.

Mr Stanley was horrified yet fascinated by the idea of a vampire at large in Liverpool, as he had always assumed that vampires were merely a figment of folklore. The Greek holy man assured him that vampires were indeed a reality and had to be taken very seriously. He explained that a vampire was the shell of a foul human being who had led a life of gross immorality and unbridled wickedness; someone who had totally rejected God, spat upon the Bible, and delighted in such abhorrent crimes as child-murder and the practice of cannibalism. Upon death, these despicable individuals were sometimes rejected from entering into the world of clean spirits, and instead became reanimated by demonic entities to wreak havoc back on earth. The Greek told Stanley dark tales of the Vyrolakos, which chilled him to the bone, and warned him to be extremely careful when passing graveyards – the lair of the Vyrolakos – during the hours of darkness.

When Cain told Stanley about the strange tomb that had been uncovered beneath his house, and the chilling inscriptions containing references to an Eastern European word which meant vampire, John Stanley's jaw dropped, but Cain tried to reassure him by saying that the whole matter was probably nothing more than a gathering of coincidences. However, thanks to the whispering of Cain's servants and the loose tongue of his friend John Stanley, the rumour of a vampire at large in south Liverpool soon became the hot topic of conversation at balls and soirées across the city. Most people took the whole thing with a pinch of salt, but when graphic, scare mongering reports of that other old sinister bogeyman of the night – Spring-Heeled Jack – were reported around the same time in the national newspapers, some people began to think that the idea of a vampire at large was not so incredible after all.

Was it all happenstance, or did a Greek vampire – a Vyrolakos – awakened from his dreamless sleep in a long-forgotten tomb, once prowl the streets of Liverpool.

The strange tomb of the Greek Vampire

Strange Bonfires

Man in bonfire

During the years which I have spent looking into matters of the supernatural, I have received numerous letters and emails from the readers of my columns and books, telling me about mysterious bonfires which they have seen at night on the outskirts of Liverpool. These reports cover a period ranging from the 1930s to the present day, and are all the more credible because they have been witnessed by people from all walks of life.

A Mr Cross, of Huyton, said that one night in about 1941 – a dreadful year for Liverpool during World War Two – two ARP wardens were livid when they spotted an enormous bonfire blazing around midnight in a field adjacent to what is now Childwall Golf Course. The two wardens set off towards the bonfire with the intention of prosecuting the careless idiots who were violating blackout regulations by lighting up the suburbs for all the Luftwaffe to see and therefore putting thousands of lives at risk.

However, when the officers came up close to the fire, they were stunned to find a circle of what looked like naked people, dancing and cavorting in a frenzy around the bonfire. Afterwards, the ARP wardens claimed that the pagan-like revellers numbered at least sixty, and events suddenly took a decidedly eerie turn when the blazing fire, and the gyrating dancers, slowly vanished before their eyes.

Strangely enough, several weeks before this bonfire incident, the ghostly figure of a long-haired woman, driving a horse-drawn chariot, was seen hurtling across that same field, and the spectral spectacle looked like something from the days of Boadicea.

In the late 1970s, police received several reports of a massive bonfire in a field close to the stretch of the M62 motorway which crosses Bowring Park. Two policemen were despatched to investigate the reports and, arriving at the site, clearly saw the silhouettes of about thirty naked men and women, holding hands and chanting something as they walked around the bonfire in an anti-clockwise direction. They cautiously approached the bonfire and as they did so they were able to distinguish some individuals amongst the revellers. Not only was one of the policemen able to recognise two of the naked 'pagans' as the couple who lived next door to him, but the other policeman also recognised someone he knew amongst the group. When the chanters spotted the two constables they immediately stopped singing and stared at them. Then, at an unseen signal, they chased them away en masse, brandishing a variety of weapons including hatchets, knives, and even a sword!

The policemen fled across the field to the relative safety of their Panda car and quickly leapt inside. Not quite sure what they had just witnessed, they drove away at high speed from nearby Sarum Road. Public disorder or not, this was one job they did not want to tackle on their own. As soon as they felt that they were at a safe distance from the bonfire, they radioed for assistance, but when they returned to the field with backup, only the glowing embers of the bonfire remained – not a single sign of the malevolent chanters.

The date of this bonfire was 30 April – a sacred date in the calendar of the Wiccan, for it is Walpurgis Night, one of the most important feasts of the year when witches and warlocks everywhere hold their Sabbat.

One of the most spectacular incidents concerning these 'witches' sabbaths' – if that is indeed what they are – took place in 1976. In July of that year, a forty-seven-year-old woman named Mrs Newnham was enjoying a quiet drink at the

Zodiac pub, off Naylorsfield Road, Childwall, at 10pm, when a child of thirteen named Michael ran into the pub in an agitated state. The lad was out of breath, not only because he had run some distance to the pub, but also because he had been frightened by the events he had witnessed. Between gasps he told Mrs Newnham that he and her twelve-year-old son had been playing football in Bowring Park, when they had noticed something very peculiar – a large gathering of weirdly dressed people dancing in the strangest way around a bonfire on a field nearby.

At first, the boys thought the whole thing was very funny and began to imitate the dancers, but the smiles soon left their faces when they realised that the people were actually killing live animals and throwing them into the flames where they writhed in agony. The killings were obviously part of some gruesome ritual or sacrifice.

Naturally the boys were sickened by the awful things they were witnessing and Michael boldly called out for them to stop what they were doing. He soon paid the price for his courage when several members of the group started to chase after him. He ran and ran but every time he looked behind, his pursuers were still there. They chased him for almost a mile before finally giving up and heading back towards the bonfire. As soon as he was sure that he had shaken them off, he headed to the pub to find Mrs Newman and tell her what had happened.

Mrs Newnham's son had been much more circumspect than his pal – he was so terrified of being spotted by the strange people that he had hidden in some undergrowth, too afraid to come out.

Mrs Newnham gulped down her drink and, with her three grown-up sons and some of their cousins in tow, set off at the trot in the direction of the field near Bowring Park, with young Michael showing them the way. It took some time to find the young lad, as he didn't dare venture out from the bushes, even when he heard their voices, but Michael was able to take them straight to him, as he hadn't moved an inch since he had left him.

The crowd around the fire had resumed their diabolical chanting and singing and seemed completely oblivious to the presence of Mrs Newnham and her sons and nephews who were gaping at the spectacle in total disbelief. Then, suddenly, all the Newnhams saw something which chilled them to the bone, something utterly horrible. There, right in the middle of the flames, was a man. At first, Mrs Newnham, having been told about the animal victims, assumed that the man was some poor soul who had been sacrificed by the fire-worshippers and she let out a cry of horror and revulsion. But what she saw next defied all rational explanation – the male figure was actually moving about with perfect ease, right in the centre of the roaring fire, somehow remaining unaffected by the terrific heat. It was as if a demonic force had been conjured up by the chanting disciples.

Mrs Newnham had seen quite enough for one night and she and her kin fled the unearthly scene as fast as their legs could carry them. The Police were informed and they investigated the event, but once again the possible Satanists had flown the scene before any arrests could take place.

The Wizard of the Calder Stones

In the seventh volume of my Haunted Liverpool series of books I related a supernatural tale featuring a strange, old, white-bearded vagrant who roamed Calderstones Park in the 1950s.

One day, in 1953, so the story goes, three thirteen-year-old local lads named Kenny, Bobby and Johnny were playing cricket in the park when the vagrant in question spoiled their game by catching the old scuffed tennis ball they were playing with after Johnny had hit it for a six. The old man then beckoned the boys to the nearby bridge on Rose Lane which looked down on to a long stretch of railway track. The vagrant saw the plume of steam from an approaching locomotive in the distance, and told the boys that he was going to throw the ball down the funnel of the train just as it was about to pass under the bridge. An instant later, when the train emerged from the other side of the bridge, the force of the escaping steam from the funnel would send the tennis ball skywards, and whoever caught it on the bridge, would one day become the most famous man in the world.

The lads were intrigued and watched as the elderly tramp did manage to hurl the ball into the locomotive's funnel as it thundered below the bridge, and the ball was indeed propelled back up by a jet of steam high into the air a split second later on the other side of the bridge. The three of them ran to grab the ball and Johnny caught it, but Kenny and Bobby laughingly questioned how their mate Johnny Lennon could ever become the most famous man in the world …

I received a plethora of letters and emails from people who not only remembered the old man of Calderstones Park – who, it turned out, was not a tramp at all – but also knew quite a lot about him. He was, allegedly, a fallen, real-life wizard who had studied alchemy in old Prague, and was highly knowledgeable in the occult sciences of High Magic and gematria. Bezzera was the name the magician was known by, but his real name remained a mystery. In the 1930s, Bezzera fell out with a lodge of fellow occultists, apparently after he supposedly succeeded in deciphering the mysterious symbols on the ancient Calder Stones, which are now housed in a special greenhouse at the park which was named after them. Bezzera is said to have rapidly descended into insanity after learning some awesome, powerful secret from the ancient stones.

In May 2005, a modern-day practising Druid got in touch with me regarding the Calderstones sorcerer, and subsequently showed me thirty-three yellowed pages of an old manuscript which had apparently once belonged to Bezzera. Upon a scrap of crumbling parchment, Bezzera had scrawled the so-called Calderstones Code: a string of thirteen numbers which no one has yet managed to decipher or make any sense of. The numbers are: 21, 26, 3, 19, 1, 30, 19, 14, 11, 10, 30, 21 and 27. I presume that the numerals of this uncrackable cipher in some way relate to the letters of the alphabet, and spell out the deadly secret. Underneath the series of numbers, the enigmatic word VULPA has been inscribed. Is this word some kind of key to the mathematical mystery? Code-breakers beware though, for some occultists believe that Bezzera deliberately encoded the secret of the ancient standing stones in the complex cipher in order to prevent unworthy minds from comprehending the mind-bending revelation of the stones.

Among the loose-leaved pages of Bezzera's notes, there are intriguing references to a type of weather control in which the self-styled magician details a series of experiments in which he exerted his powerful 'mental energy' to dissolve fair weather cumulus clouds over the Lake District and Liverpool in the summers of 1932 and 1933.

Bezzera's attempts at psychokinetic weather control are strikingly similar to the experiments of Dr Rolf Alexander, a New Zealand psychic known as 'The Cloudbuster' because he could apparently disperse clouds simply by concentrating his mind on them. Bezzera states in his manuscript that 'Magins [initiated magicians] of antiquity could stop the earth spinning on its axis, creating unusually long nights or days, depending on whether the sun or the stars were in the sky when the world was stopped in its rotation. It is recorded that in the reign of the Emperor Yao, the sun did not set for a full ten days, and entire forests were ignited by the stationary sun causing widespread destruction. Also, in the Book of Joshua, it was written that the sun stood still in the midst of heaven and did not go down for a whole day.'

Bezzera's manuscript also details experiments for practical magic which could be used for conjuring up storms and plagues of flies, or frogs and stones to annoy an enemy, and refers to the sky-borne plagues of frogs, gnats, flies and locusts that swept the land of Ramses II in the Old Testament. Strangely enough, Bezzera wrote about the conjuration of these plagues in June 1932. It is curious that upon Saturday, 18 June 1932, the Liverpool Evening Express newspaper contained a report with the headlines:

CLOUD OF FLIES – Window and Car Windscreens Covered.

The article told of how dense swarms of small flies had suddenly descended on various parts of Liverpool. In some streets the swarms were so thick that windows were blackened and the windscreens of motorcars were thickly covered. The flies arrived in vast clouds and caused a major inconvenience to both pedestrians and motorists alike. One motorist told an Evening Express reporter that when he was driving along Lime Street the windscreen of his car became so thickly covered with the flies that he could scarcely see where he was going. He was forced to stop and wipe them off before he could proceed on his journey any further.

Professor W S Patton, Professor of Entomology at Liverpool University, told an Evening Express reporter that the insects were known as Ichneumon flies – small parasitic wasps which do not bite. Professor Patton said that it was impossible, without investigation, to state where the flies had come from, or why they were swarming in such great numbers.

Curiouser still, in the following year, the Liverpool Echo reported on Saturday, 20 May 1933, with the headlines:

SANDSTORM ON MERSEYSIDE – Amazing Weather Phenomenon – Tennis Players Rush from Hail of Pebbles.

The article described how the weather had been in the most freakish of moods on Merseyside on that afternoon, and there had been great apprehension amongst the crowds watching the Liverpool annual May parade of horses, when, at about 3.30pm, continuous black clouds began to roll across the sky.

> About 3.30pm an amazing phenomenon took place. A great brown cloud of what appeared to be mist suddenly appeared from the river, and, sweeping down all the main streets, caught pedestrians unprepared.
>
> It was a whirlwind of dust and tiny particles of stone, which swept along at a terrific pace. Shop blinds flapped loudly, windows and doors slammed open or banged shut, and hundreds of people were temporarily blinded.

It was all over within two minutes, but in its wake came curious changes in the atmosphere. The low clouds, which promised rain, suddenly began to whirl and boil as though in a vacuum created by the low wind, and then gradually welded together and went higher. The threatened rain held off, and at twenty minutes after the first blast, the sun burst through once again.

The great bulk of St George's Hall acted as a very effective shield for the majority of the spectators at the May parade, but thousands in William Brown Street got the full effect of the dust storm.

'Reports from the districts indicate that the dust cloud was widespread. At Port Sunlight Recreation Ground it swept across about five minutes before Liverpool experienced it.

A cloud of dust, sand and pebbles struck tennis players there, many of whom, as they rushed for shelter, were temporarily blinded by the storm, which only lasted two minutes. "I have never seen anything like it in this country before," said a tennis player after he had dashed for shelter.

There was a stampede for shelter as the storm burst with remarkable suddenness. It was preluded by a dense blackness overhead, which put an end to the tennis playing, and then came the dust.

Small pebbles, mixed with the sand and grit, struck the face with stinging effect, and there was a general shrieking of frightened children. Then the storm subsided as quickly as it had arisen, and the blue in the sky reappeared.

At 3.30pm the sandstorm was reported at Norris Green. Here it resembled a whirlwind, and left a train of broken slates, split window blinds, and shattered blooms in many gardens. Mr Hugh Semple, of 126 Utting Avenue East, said he was blown off his bicycle by a sudden gust over the district with remarkable ferocity.

It stripped the slates off the corners of Corporation

> houses like leaves from a tree, and left gaping holes in roofs. A child's perambulator was overturned, but fortunately the baby did not appear to have been hurt, while close by a tradesman's hand van was also blown over.
>
> The Calday Grange Grammar Schools sports had to be suspended for nearly half an hour due to the sandstorm.

Meteorologists were at a loss to explain these freak weather incidents documented in the local newspapers. Could it be possible that they were conjured up by the Wizard of the Calderstones?

By the end of the 1930s, Bezzera had become an introspective recluse at his suburban home in the Woolton Park area of Liverpool. The lodge of magicians with whom Bezzera had fallen out with claimed that Winston Churchill had considered enlisting the services of covens across the land to use Black Magic as a weapon against Adolf Hitler, who, some maintained, was a malevolent wizard himself, who had abused his powers to mesmerise millions of his fellow countrymen. Bezzera predicted that Hitler, like many false Messiahs before him, would soon 'reap the whirlwind' for his evil acts. The swastika, hijacked by the Nazis as their own logo, was an ancient occult symbol, last used by members of the Hermetic Order of the Golden Dawn – a secret sect founded in the late nineteenth century. Friedrich Krohn, a Sternberg dentist, and a student of the Occult, first suggested the swastika as a symbol to an astrology-fixated Hitler in the 1920s. The twin lightning strike symbol used by the SS was also another ancient esoteric symbol plundered by the Nazis, according to Bezzera.

The huge gatherings of chanting soldiers at the Nuremberg rallies, presided over by Adolf Hitler, were not just carried out as a propaganda exercise to be captured by newsreels throughout the world, but, according to occultists, the unprecedented mass assemblies actually fulfilled the criteria for the so-called 'Cone of Power' ritual. During the rallies, which were held at night, a ring of gigantic searchlights encircling Hitler projected mile-long beams of light which rose to form a cone with its apex in the night sky, centred on the ranting Austrian below.

The Lodge asked Bezzera to participate in the old Wiccan Cone of Power ritual, which would be focused against Hitler, who was threatening to invade Britain any day soon. It is said that in the past, Wiccans had deployed the awesome might of the Cone of Power upon would-be invaders of Albion, with devastating results. The Spanish Armada was wrecked by mysterious violent storms before it was able to reach England's shores, and Napoleon's disastrous plans for an invasion of our country were similarly attributed to the powerful Wiccan ritual.

The Cone of Power ritual went ahead, without Bezzera, in the New Forest, in the summer of 1940. Some accounts say that the ritual took place on the Wiccan day of Lammas (1 August). Close to the historical Rufus Stone, a circle measuring nine feet in diameter was traced on the ground, and in its centre a pile of brushwood was ignited. Nearby stood a lantern. Encircling the fire, a coven of naked witches chanted things I could never reveal, and amongst these Wiccans, was one local man, Gerald Gardner of Blundellsands, in Crosby, hailed today as the world-famous father of modern witchcraft.

To enable the Cone to exert its full and devastating effect on Hitler, a sacrifice was deemed necessary, and so two of the older witches agreed not to coat themselves in greasy animal fat which would normally insulate them from the cold of the night when they were stripped naked. Even though it was a summer's night, the atmosphere that night seemed glacial.

The deadly rite was duly carried out, and soon afterwards, the two old witches passed away, perhaps not entirely from hypothermia, but rather through the draining of their life-forces. The occultists claimed that the ritual was a major success, and that the tide of war turned against Hitler from that moment on, as a direct result of their efforts.

The ostracised Bezzera spent his twilight years wandering the streets of Liverpool wearing ragged clothes, his ivory beard long and unkempt and his rheumy eyes opaque with cataracts. Bemused children and outraged citizens would often watch him as he chalked elaborate symbols of the moon and stars on the pavement near the gates of Calderstones Park and wonder what they could mean. To the uniformed rangers, whose job it was to keep undesirables out of the park, Bezzera was something of a nuisance and they tried to ban him from the park.

The exact time and place of Bezzera's death are unknown, and the full details of his life remain equally sketchy.

The Berwyn Explosions

At around 8.35pm on the Wednesday night of 23 January 1974 a succession of red, green and white lights were seen in the skies by the captains and crews of several ships out in the Irish Sea. None of the observers had ever seen anything like them before and they all agreed that the strange lights were moving too far too quickly, and at too great an altitude, to be ships' flares, and the same steady, multi-coloured, sparkling lights had been seen seconds earlier by coastguards in Scotland, as they travelled southwards across the sky.

At around 8.37pm, police stations on the Isle of Man were besieged with frantic telephone calls from anxious islanders who had also witnessed the mysterious lights passing overhead. At around the same time, the coastguards of Cumbria, Lancashire, Merseyside and Wirral had also sighted the lights, which now seemed to be predominantly of a greenish hue. The Angelsey coastguards caught sight of the lights seconds before they descended into northern Wales.

Then, at precisely 8.39pm, a fierce explosion, three miles south of Llandrillo, Clwyd, rocked the whole of North Wales, Wirral, Cheshire and Lancashire. At Edinburgh University's Seismology Department, earthquake experts stated that the mysterious blast had caused a tremor 'which was substantial in the history of the country'. The magnitude of the tremor was 3.5 to 4 on the Richter scale, and this data was corroborated by other seismological readings recorded on the instruments based at the Geological Science's observatory at Eskdale, Eskdalemuir.

Gwynedd police received numerous eye-witness reports of an object, initially assumed to be a meteorite, coming slowly down to earth in a ball of flames and exploding just before impact on the 2,572 foot-high Cader Bronwen mountain, near Llandrillo. Not only were the switchboards of the emergency services of the entire North West swamped with telephone calls, some people also rang their local newspapers with accounts of the perplexing events they had seen.

Thomas McDonnel, a fifty-two-year-old resident of Bridge Farm Close on the Woodchurch Estate in Birkenhead, contacted the Liverpool Echo and gave them a vivid description of a fiery object that he had observed in the sky over Wales at 11.15pm on that same night. "I had just got off the train at Upton Station when I saw it. It seemed to explode and a kind of white substance seemed to flow off it. It was moving very slowly," said Mr McDonnel, who said he had never seen anything like it before in his life. And therein lies yet another mysterious aspect of the exploding meteorite; lights and aerial explosions were still being seen in the skies over Wales almost three hours after the initial impact had taken place.

People in Chester, Wrexham, Caernarvon, Corwen, Liverpool and Birkenhead saw the same enigmatic coloured lights drifting through the night sky after the impact of the so-called meteorite. Nevertheless, a subsequent intensive search of Cader Bronwen and the rest of the Berwyn mountains failed to unearth a single trace of meteoric debris. Then came mysterious reports of a military cover-up; it was said that a huge UFO had impacted into the Berwyn Mountains, and that the Army had cordoned off the crash site and had even warned the police to keep away. Bizarrely enough, days after the strange 'meteorite' explosion, the Ministry of Defence informed the Press that the whole incident had been caused by an RAF photo-flash night bombing exercise over Wales. However, the hundreds of people who had seen the coloured lights in the sky – from Scottish coastguards and Manx policemen to witnesses in Lancashire, Wirral and Angelsey, were unconvinced. They were adamant that the strange, high-altitude objects they had seen could not possibly have been caused by some RAF exercise in darkest Wales – there had to be some other explanation.

It would seem, therefore, that a high-level cover-up did take place – but for what reason? Was it, perhaps, because the military powers of the United Kingdom considered that there would be wide-scale panic amongst the population if it became known that a spacecraft from another planet had crashed in Wales?

Two years after this mystifying incident, an equally baffling crash took place in the same location in North Wales. On the Friday night of 6 August 1976, an explosion was heard over a ten-mile radius. The deafening boom was preceded by an intense explosion of light which continued to illuminate the night skies for several miles for a duration of some three minutes. On this occasion, coloured lights in the sky were observed both before and after the explosion, travelling over Cheshire, Lancashire, Merseyside and Wirral. On this occasion, the RAF did not claim responsibility for the incident, but some experts did blame the supersonic airliner Concord, claiming that the tremendous bang was nothing more than the aircraft's sonic boom. However, this theory was soon dismissed, as the plane had not even been in the air at the time.

The 1974 and 1976 explosions therefore remain a complete mystery.

Scary Mary of Scotland Road

When the police moved their archived criminal files from St Anne Street to Canning Place, many years ago, a large number of their records were lost in transit. The files pertaining to the unsolved murder of Madge Kirby in 1908 were among the misplaced documents, and many other intriguing cases of old Liverpool were also either mislaid, or even accidentally destroyed, during the relocation to the new police headquarters.

The sinister case of 'Scary Mary' of Scotland Road is another one of these police files that has sadly gone astray, but luckily, through painstaking research, I have been able to piece together some of the curious facts of this long forgotten incident.

At three o'clock on the freezing Friday morning of 15 January 1892, police constables Jones and Black were proceeding on the their beat along Scotland Road. Their progress was marked by the steady crunch of their black regulation boots on the ankle-deep crust of frozen snow which covered the pavements. Although a full moon was lighting up the deserted streets more than adequately, the policemen had the bull's eye lanterns on their belts lit, because they at least provided a little warmth.

As the men of the law trudged past Horatio Street, they came across the solitary figure of a woman, silhouetted in the silvery moonlit snow. She was obviously enraged about something because she was hurling snowballs at an unseen object in the sky, and cursing the moon with decidedly unladylike profanities in a suspiciously masculine-sounding voice. As the policemen crept closer to the demented woman the bemused looks on their moustached faces betrayed their consternation. From closer quarters they could clearly see that the irate person was not a woman after all. No, 'she' was most definitely a man and a hefty one at that, although dressed as a woman. He was aiming his snowballs at the moon, for what purpose they could not imagine.

Laughter suddenly rang out from a nearby doorway, startling the crazed female impersonator. He turned to look at a cackling drunk who was slouched on the steps of a house clutching a bottle of rum. The mad drag artist then noticed constables Jones and Black, and immediately tried to run off, but slipped instead on ice. His black straw bonnet slipped off in the fall, revealing what was obviously a long-haired wig on the man's head.

The policemen found the whole incident amusing, something to take their mind off the penetrating cold, and they smiled at each other as they bent down to apprehend the cross-dressing oddball, whom they assumed to be one of the many rootless inadequates who roamed the city's streets. They were in for a nasty shock. The man swiftly produced a knife and a cosh from under his feminine robes and stabbed Constable Black in the armpit and then knocked Jones clean out with one blow to the forehead. As his parting shot, he then kicked Black in the crotch for good measure. Having dusted himself down and picked up his bonnet, he screamed something unintelligible at the two policemen, and ran off towards Cazneau Street, where he quickly vanished into the warren of dingy streets and alleyways, which had proved a useful escape route for many a villain before him.

Black clutched a handful of icy snow and patted it on to the face of his unconscious colleague, in an effort to revive him, but he was out stone cold. The drunk staggered over and kindly offered Black his rum bottle, from which the policeman took a grateful swig. By now blood was trickling into the snow from his underarm wound, which throbbed painfully. Black blew loudly on his whistle, and before the policeman from the neighbouring beat came running to his aid, the drunken Samaritan informed the wounded copper that the assailant was known as 'Scary Mary' to the people in the neighbourhood – an unknown madman who dressed as a female by night, in which garb he went on the prowl through the streets of Liverpool.

One evening, a week later, two young women, Annie Davies and Collette Flaherty, were making their way home when they were attacked and slashed by a knife-wielding man who was dressed as a woman. The attack took place just after 11pm on Roscommon Street, just two hundred yards from the scene of the previous assault on the two policemen. Despite being deeply traumatised by the ordeal, in her witness statement Miss Davies was able to give a very good description of their attacker. She described how he had worn a black crepe bonnet beneath which his contorted face looked ghastly and evil. His most distinctive feature was his dark, thick eyebrows which met in the middle. His face was plastered with thick make-up and he was dressed in women's clothes, but neither the make-up nor the clothes was sufficient to disguise the fact that he was a man.

A few days after the attack on the two women, Scary Mary struck again, this time at midnight on Silvester Street, and once again the target of the assault was a female – a married woman in her sixties named Joan Aspinall. On this occasion the attack was even more ferocious – Mary leapt out of the shadows and confronted her victim. She drew a long, sword-like blade from a scabbard which was disguised as an umbrella. She took several swipes at Mrs Aspinall, who screamed in terror and then fainted in the snow from the shock. Fortunately, a night watchman heard her cries of terror and rushed to her aid. He sounded the alarm on his whistle, and Mary ran off into the night, disappearing as she had before into the maze of alleyways.

Not surprisingly, the three attacks caused great alarm amongst the local population and Captain J W Nott Bower, Head Constable of the Central Police Office, drafted in extra police and plain-clothed officers to the area where Scary Mary was known to operate. Two detectives were chosen to co-ordinate the intensive hunt for the mentally unstable knifeman, but their exhaustive enquiries resulted in no success whatsoever.

In response to the attacks, at the Fail-Me-Never public house on Vauxhall Road, a local entrepreneurial rogue named Sydney O'Brien started selling a range of 'life-preserving coshes' and lead-knobbed sticks to the customers, so that they could defend themselves against Scary Mary. Sydney's slow-witted sidekick, 'Loggerhead', a bald, 6 foot 7 inch giant of a man with a distinctive butterfly tattoo on his forehead, coerced drinkers with menacing strong-arm tactics to purchase the coshes and sticks.

In another local pub – The Brown Cow on Juvenal Street – the landlord boasted that he had purchased two pistols – one for himself and one for his wife – and they intended to use them if the psychopath dressed like a pantomime dame crossed their paths.

As hysteria mounted on the streets of Scotland Road, false alarms and scare stories sent ripples of fear through the community. On 14 February of that year – St Valentine's Day – a young policeman walking his beat on Eldon Street was waylaid by a gang of ragged children who urged him to go and arrest Scary Mary, because she was smashing windows and threatening to cut people up just around the corner. The policeman, barely out of his teens, knew all about the terrifying reputation of Mary – the attack on his two colleagues was a frequent topic of conversation down at the station – and so he took a deep breath, and took out his whistle, ready to summon assistance.

However, when he turned the corner into Limekiln Lane, whistle in one hand and truncheon in the other, he came across a rather portly, middle-aged drunk he knew well – Polly O'Shaughnessy – one of the area's colourful, though harmless, characters. Polly was surrounded by a semi-circle of bemused bystanders as she systematically smashed the window panes of a house with a soot-blackened poker. It turned out that Polly, in a highly intoxicated state, had imagined that she had seen the face of the husband who had deserted her years before, in the windows of the house next door to hers. The young policeman wrestled the poker out of her hands before arresting her and taking her into custody.

By the spring of 1893, the unit in charge of the case had narrowed down their list of suspects, and the handful of people were kept under close observation until they were all were eliminated, all except one; a hairdresser named Foley, who had lodgings at a house on Everton Brow.

At 10.30pm on the Sunday evening of 13 March 1893 – the night of a full moon – some plain-clothed policemen watched as Foley left the house, via the back alleyway, dressed in female attire. Foley gazed up at the window of the house from where he was being observed, and immediately stopped dead in his tracks. He somehow seemed to sense that he was being watched and he turned on his heels and walked back to the house. One of the detectives in charge of the case, a man called Parkinson, ordered his officers to storm the house at once, convinced that he had finally got his man. They tried the front and back doors of the house but they were firmly bolted, and when the police finally managed to gain entry, they found their quarry trembling under a dining table in an insensible state, still wearing the women's clothing.

One of the other lodgers came downstairs to complain about the noise wearing only his pyjamas, and when the officers of the law explained the situation, the lodger said he was deeply shocked; as far as he was concerned, the chap was totally innocent. The landlady of the house tried to prevent the arrest of Foley, arguing that he was a harmless, slow-witted man – he wouldn't hurt a fly, never mind go around attacking people. Two policemen took lengthy statements from the landlady and the other lodgers in the house, and the feeble-minded suspect was taken to the Central Police Office at 111 Dale Street to be interrogated.

On the following morning detectives eventually established that the forlorn figure whom they had taken into custody was not Foley after all – but a mentally retarded man who was related to the landlady. Foley evidently must have dressed the unfortunate soul in female clothes and then gone to bed in the hope of framing him.

Captain Nott Bower visited the framed man in his cell at the bridewell and turning to Detective Parkinson said, "All of the descriptions of the wanted man mentioned eyebrows that join in the middle; do this man's eyebrows meet in the middle? Do they?"

Detective Parkinson shook his head defeatedly.

"No, Sir," he answered, sheepishly.

"Precisely!" fumed the Captain, furious at the bumbling detective's lack of success in apprehending Scary Mary. "This poor wretch is totally innocent. Escort him back to his relative's house at once, and see that he is given something more suitable to wear than that ridiculous garb!"

"Yes, Sir. Sorry, Sir," said Parkinson, his head still low.

Despite an intensive manhunt in the Scotland Road area, the elusive Mr Foley was never caught, although he did have the audacity to return to the night streets of Liverpool once more in the October and November of that year – and on both occasions he was at large on the night of a full moon, although he did not try to harm anyone on those final occasions.

On the night of 6 October, Mary was seen gazing through a window at a widow in the backyard of a house on Rokeby Street. The woman glanced up from her needlework to be confronted by the heavily made-up face staring at her with a devilish smile through the window, and she let out a scream. The creepy transvestite fled at once and was heard scrambling over the backyard wall.

On 4 November, there was a report of a similar incident at a house on Gerard Street, and on this occasion, two men chased after the peeping Tom, but they lost sight of him somewhere in dark alleyways of the Islington district and had to give up the chase.

After that final incident, Scary Mary was never seen, or heard from again, but some of the superstitious folk of Scotland Road still claim that upon certain nights, when the moon is full and casts its silvery glow over the neighbourhood, the prowling ghost of Scary Mary may still be seen prowling about their streets …

The Speke Birdman

Leo Valentin

It was Monday 21 May 1956 and the sky over Speke Airport was a blindingly hot azure canopy, unseasonably warm for that time of year. Thousands of feet below, large excited crowds of people were milling about, having gathered at the airfield to watch the famous French Bird Man or Homme Oiseau make one of his spectacular, freefall, parachute jumps. Until recent years, when Leo Valentin had begun his freefall flights, flying men were merely the stuff of Greek myths in most people's minds. Nearly everyone had heard the story of Icarus, the ancient careless birdman of Greek legend, who flew too close to the sun and plunged to the ground. The feathered wings which Icarus wore were held together with wax and when he flew too close to the sun, the wax started to melt with dramatic results: the wings fell apart, and he plummeted to his death.

That was many centuries ago, but this was now the Jet Age, and this Bird Man had already forged a formidable reputation for himself by successfully jumping from aeroplanes in flight, using nothing more elaborate than a pair of homemade balsa wings to see him safely back down to the ground. Without a doubt, many of the hundreds of expectant people squinting skywards on that hot May afternoon regarded the courageous winged Frenchman as a pioneer of a coming era – an era which had been promised within the pages of futuristic comics such as The Eagle.

Instead of Dan Dare, the pilot of the future upon this day was thirty-seven-year-old dare-devil Frenchman, Leo Valentin, and he had promised his increasingly anxious friends and family that this was definitely to be his last flight. He had been risking life and limb experimenting with unaided winged flight since 1947, and had recently decided that it was high time for him to 'hang up his wings' and pursue a safer occupation.

Before Valentin had taken to the air, parachutists had simply tumbled chaotically out of planes, literally on a wing and a prayer, clutching their handles in a sort of tuck position. Their most fervent hope was that they wouldn't get tangled up in the cords of their parachutes. It was Valentin who perfected the art of freefall, and everyone thought he was completely mad when, in 1947, he successfully completed the world's first freefall parachute jump from a height of nine thousand feet. After making his first, conventional parachute jump on 15 October 1938, when the sport was virtually unheard of in France, Valentin had been determined to show the world that he could learn to fall in a stable position.

However, after the successful 1947 jump he also spoke of the fear which he had experienced during the fall. Fear is a natural human instinct when a person is removed from his natural environment, and is at the cutting edge of physical achievement.

"I experience a moment of absolute panic, a panic of my whole being, something resembling the primordial fear of the caveman ... here I am, feeling a fear that I had never known before ... It is ridiculous! I open without a hitch at one thousand five hundred feet."

On that same day in 1947 Valentin made a second jump from nine thousand feet and this time, having proved that freefall was possible, he was far more confident and able to enjoy the intense sensations of freedom and pleasure which drive men to experiment in an element which is alien to earthbound creatures.

"An hour later we take off again ... suddenly I have a sensation of great well-being. Had it not been for the wind I might be motionless in the sky, reclining face downward on the cushions of air through which I am plunging, almost without stirring. It is so different from the normal twisting that for a moment I am scared. It seems impossible that it can be so easy, so agreeable, so intoxicating in its smoothness.

"This revelation leaves me at one and the same time numb and yet deeply moved in spirit. There is no reason why one should not fall like this until the end of time, in an element whose sense of lightness no adjective can conjure up. How wonderful it would be to fall asleep in this state of ineffable ease."

He achieved many records and became one of the most celebrated 'Hommes Oiseaux', employing a succession of radical designs using both flexible and rigid wings. He invented the skydiver's now familiar belly-down frog position to control his descent, and yet, as the above quote testifies, the Frenchman was prone to sudden, mid-air panic attacks. Plummeting to earth at a speed of over one hundred and twenty miles per hour, he would often momentarily freeze before tremblingly reaching for the ripcord, just in the nick of time.

Ridiculous as it may seem for such a daring pioneer, Valentin also suffered from recurring nightmares, in which he was falling to his death, and his whole life, and particularly his flying, was ruled by superstition. Absolutely no one was allowed to touch the bright orange wings of balsa wood that he strapped on before a jump – his life depended on them and he could trust no one but himself. He felt compelled to shout the words, "One, two, three!" immediately prior to every jump he ever did, and when he came to Liverpool he demanded to be given room one hundred and twenty-three at the hotel at which he was staying.

One of the many excited children assembled at Speke airfield to watch the display on that beautiful spring day was thirteen-year-old Wavertree schoolboy, John Molyneux. To him, like many of the other children who had been brought along by their parents, this special day out had been looked forward to for the picnic, treats and carnival atmosphere, as much as for the aerial display. When Leo Valentin finally made his jump John was preoccupied batting mayflies and wasps away from the delicious ice cream cornet he was eating. Suddenly he heard his friend's mother scream – a scream that was taken up by virtually every other adult in the crowd.

John had watched with fascination as the plane had roared down the runway and taken off, but had lost interest as it had made its slow ascent to nine thousand feet, so he had not noticed when Valentin had jumped out of the plane. When John heard the screams he instinctively looked up, craning his neck to focus on the plane. He soon located it and then noticed a tiny speck just underneath it and to one side. It was the Bird Man, tumbling haphazardly through the sky, thousands of feet above the ground. Valentin's wings had clipped the plane as he jumped, instantly sending him into an uncontrollable downward spin. Those with binoculars watched with bated breath as he pulled frantically at the ripcord. He tried time after time but the lines had become entangled around the orange balsa wood wings and his parachute could not be activated.

Even with their scant knowledge of how the day's events should have unfolded, the spectators down below, even without the help of binoculars, immediately sensed that the jump was not going according to plan – something had gone horribly wrong – and a shiver of impending disaster swept through the crowd. Women shielded their children's eyes and turned them away from the tragedy being played out above the airfield. The women looked away themselves as the Frenchman's body gradually changed from a tiny dot into a discernable human being – a human being whose last seconds on earth were rapidly ebbing away as he plunged ever more quickly to the ground. What terrible thoughts were going through the poor man's mind can only be imagined.

John Molyneux dropped his ice cream cone and froze, not because of the Frenchman's fate, but because Valentin seemed to be falling in his direction and he was frightened that he was going to be crushed by his body. People around him began to run away in panic, fanning out in every direction, glancing up every few seconds to check on Valentin's descent. But the schoolboy stood rooted to the spot, unable to move, his legs numb with fear.

Wave upon wave of horrified screams rose up from the crowd – all the spectators felt so helpless as they watched the awful scene unfold. Although Valentin was now hurtling towards the ground and certain death at a tremendous speed, for most people those last few seconds seemed to be played out in slow motion. There was absolutely nothing that anyone could do to save the doomed Frenchman – this was to be, as he had promised his loved ones – his last flight.

John stood statue still as the silhouette of Leo Valentin, wings spread like an eagle, plunged relentlessly downwards, landing with a sickening dull thud, about two hundred yards away from where he was standing.

Valentin had impacted into a field of grain at the side of the airfield, and

John hurried over to the spot with a group of men. The lifeless body was lying face down, in a tangle of lines and splintered wings. Valentin's recurrent nightmare had come true. Two of the men gently overturned the body – it was obvious that he was dead but John noticed that Leo Valentin had a peaceful smile on his face and that his eyes were closed, as if he were sleeping. Despite the later news reports, he had suffered no appalling injuries, and there was not a trace of blood to be found on his body. John was led away back to his mother as the men fittingly covered the fallen Bird Man with his silk parachute.

Leo Valentin's pioneering and courageous freefall flights had a profound effect on the sport of parachuting and today, the great man's grandson, Francois 'Leo' LeCloux, has taken up the mantle and is making spectacular progress. I wonder whether he will follow in his famous grandfather's footsteps and push the boundaries of the sport still further.

The Mystery of John Conway

John Conway

Bridgewater Street, which runs from the once-busy waterfront thoroughfare of Chaloner Street to Jamaica Street, formed part of a bustling Celtic ghetto in late Victorian times. The area around Rutter Street in Toxteth, nicknamed 'Gerry Hill', had a high concentration of Irish settlers who had been arriving in Liverpool from Ireland since the days of the first year of the Great Starvation in 1845, but further north in the Toxteth district, there existed a caucus of Irish, Scottish and Welsh people who regarded all English-speaking 'outsiders' with suspicion and deep-rooted mistrust.

The secretive clans of this area of the city spoke almost exclusively in Gaelic, and had no respect for the ruling monarch of the day – Queen Victoria – the 'Famine Queen', who had done nothing when more than a million Irish men, women and children died of starvation and the subsequent diseases of cholera and typhus between the years of 1845 and 1851.

Surprisingly, during those horrific famine years, Ireland actually produced a bumper crop of oats, wheat, barley and vegetables, yet this food of the land was not used to feed the starving Irish. This was because the majority of farmers in Ireland were tenant-cultivators and they had to go on paying their rents, even when the main potato crop had failed, and so were forced to sell their other crops to raise the money. Few people were aware that Queen Victoria personally donated five thousand pounds towards the various Irish famine relief programmes, but her donation was but a drop in the ocean and did nothing to alleviate the disaster.

By the 1870s, the monarchy had fallen further out of favour with the Irish people, mostly because Victoria refused to visit Ireland in protest at the decision of Dublin Corporation's refusal to congratulate her son, the Prince of Wales, on his marriage to Princess Alexandra of Denmark. Nor were the Irish forthcoming in congratulating the royal couple on the birth of their eldest son, Prince Albert Victor.

There were eight attempts to assassinate Queen Victoria during her long reign, and four of these efforts were Irish in origin.

In June 1887, the Clan-na-Gael (a secret society of Irish Fenians) in New York, hatched a daring plot to blow up the Queen and the rest of the Royal Family, along with most of the British Cabinet at Westminster Abbey, during the monarch's Golden Jubilee commemoration service. Days before the daring assassination was to take place, Scotland Yard claimed that it had captured the Irish dynamiters – who had come into Britain through Liverpool Docks – but the main conspirator, ringleader General Francis Millen, managed to escape and fled abroad. The Fenians were tried, found guilty of attempting to murder the Queen, her family, and the British Government, and they were sentenced to harsh penal servitude for life.

The Queen felt deeply indebted to the detectives at Scotland Yard for the action they had taken to thwart the conspiracy, and she also praised the Prime Minister Lord Salisbury for saving her life. What the monarch did not know was that the entire plot to assassinate her had actually been masterminded by the British Government and Lord Salisbury! Furthermore, sinister letters linked the infamous Fenians to Charles Parnell and other Irish MPs who had been pressing for Home Rule for Ireland. The letters were forgeries, penned by Dublin journalist Richard Pigott, and sold to The Times newspaper. The letters were subsequently exposed for what they were, and the public realised that someone in high power was going to enormous and fraudulent lengths in an attempt to destroy Parnell, and with him, the possibility of Home Rule for Ireland.

During this period of political turmoil regarding the question of Irish independence, the Fenians had bases in Liverpool, and many members of the Clan-na-Gael spoke Gaelic, which brings us back to Liverpool's Bridgewater Street, in 1891; for in that street, in that year, there lodged a highly regarded, hard-working Irishman of sixty-one years of age, known as John Conway. He was a man with strong political views, which were undoubtedly pro-Fenian, and he spoke in the alien tongue of Gaelic to like-minded people and fellow countrymen. The dark-bearded, bowler-hatted Mr Conway worked as a full-time official delegate of the Seamen's and Firemen's Trade Union, and carried with him an air of respectability due to his erect bearing and fine attire.

Late one evening, in May 1891, a nine-year-old boy called Nicholas Martin was out playing on the streets of Toxteth. It was nearly dark and the gas lamps had already been lit but his parents felt that he was perfectly safe playing in the street with his friends. Nicholas ran to pick up a ball and suddenly noticed a well-dressed figure standing underneath one of the glowing lamp-posts and the figure beckoned to him. John Conway started chatting to Nicholas about the game he was playing, asking about the rules, the number of people who could play and so on. Using that age-old tactic of the promise of sweets, Conway then managed to lure young Nicholas back to his office on Stanhope Street. As they made their way there many witnesses noticed the young boy and the old man walking along together through the gaslit evening streets – streets which Nicholas Martin would never see again.

Three days later, Nicholas Martin had still not returned to his Toxteth home and his frantic parents were out of their mind with worry. They and their friends and neighbours had searched the entire neighbourhood but could find no trace of Nicholas and they were beginning to fear that something dreadful had befallen their beloved son. That night, three days after his disappearance, the missing boy's father opened the Liverpool Echo hoping to read of something which might give some clue as to his whereabouts. He recoiled in horror as he read a deeply disturbing report of the discovery of a male child's mutilated body which had been found inside a canvas sailor's bag, floating in the Sandon Dock.

A feeling of hopeless dread overwhelmed Mr Martin and he immediately sensed that the boy's body was that of Nicholas, even though every fibre of his body fought against such an idea. He went straight to the police station from where he was escorted to the mortuary to identify what turned out to be the hacked up remains of his missing son. The boy's body had been extensively mutilated with a knife, and his lower legs had been sawn off at the knees in order to fit the corpse into the canvas bag. The saw and the knife which had been used on the boy, were also found in the bag.

His worst fears confirmed, Mr Martin broke down and cried. Who on earth would want to do such a thing to his innocent, beautiful son? The poor child's throat had been deeply sliced, and there were crazed stab and slash wounds all over his body – obviously the work of a maniac.

The only clue which the detectives had to work on was the distinctive sailor's bag in which the body had been found, and they quickly set to work searching for any seamen's outfitters, or second-hand stores, which might have sold such a bag.

Within twenty-four hours, diligent detective work brought about a breakthrough after a routine enquiry at a Mrs Mary Patterson's second-hand clothes shop on Park Road. Mrs Patterson had no trouble identifying the bag as the one that had been bought recently by a bearded old man who seemed to live locally. Armed with a detailed description of this elderly man, the police set about making house to house enquiries – a job that was impeded somewhat by the distrustful Gaelic-speaking people of the neighbourhood, who regarded anyone in authority with deep mistrust.

Their painstaking enquiries finally led the policemen to the house on Bridgewater Street where John Conway was a lodger, and the detectives realised immediately that he was a perfect fit for the description of the man they were looking for. They arrested him on the spot and called on Mrs Patterson to identify him as the man who had recently purchased the sailor's bag. She did so without hesitation, but Conway, who admitted that he had bought the bag, claimed he had bought it on behalf of a mysterious Norwegian.

Detectives then visited Conway's office on Stanhope Street and discovered bloodstains in the attic room of the premises. Conway was unable to explain the damning evidence, nor could he refute the testimony of several reliable witnesses who had come forward to testify that they had seen him walking along with Nicholas Martin on the night of his disappearance.

The father of the murder victim, already deeply traumatised by his son's horrific murder, was further shocked to discover that he actually knew the perpetrator, John Conway – he had lodged with his family fourteen years earlier in nearby Blundell Street – only in those days, the murder suspect had gone under the name of John Hooper, and he had told the Martins that he had just returned from Australia.

On the basis of the accumulated evidence, John Conway was charged with the murder of Nicholas Martin and the subsequent trial at St George's Hall drew a record number of sightseers – far greater than the crowds who had flocked to the hall when Florence Maybrick was on trial there three years before. They thronged around the great hall, jostling and jockeying for position, each hoping to catch a glimpse of the infamous John Conway and following all the twists and turns of the trial with gory interest. People who knew Conway spoke very well of him and claimed that he was the sort of man who wouldn't hurt a fly. It was certainly true that the accused had no criminal record, or any previous history of violent behaviour. All the same, the witnesses who had seen Conway with the boy on the night of his disappearance, gave their testimony in front of the jury, who took just twenty-five minutes to return a verdict of guilty.

Upon word of the eagerly awaited verdict leaking out of the court, thousands sent up a cheer outside St George's Hall – on the steps, between the gargantuan pillars, and upon the crowded plateau. The twentieth day of August was the date set for the execution at Kirkdale Gaol.

On the day before the hanging, the executioner, James Berry, arrived in Liverpool, and immediately offended the local populace by his unprofessional conduct. He joked about Conway and even sang a parody of a well-known ballad which alluded to the forthcoming hanging of the senior citizen turned child-killer. On the same day, in the privacy of his cell in Kirkdale prison, Conway finally confessed his dreadful crime to the Catholic Chaplain, Father Bronte, and also attempted to explain the motive behind the murder. He was at great pains to assure Bronte that he had not sexually abused the child before or after he had killed him.

"I protest that my motive was not outrage," Conway said, morosely. "Such a thought I never in all my life entertained."

The priest, who was no stranger to such last minute confessions, made the sign of the cross and encouraged the condemned man to go on with his confession – his salvation depended on it.

"Drink has been my ruin, not lust," continued Conway. "I was impelled to the crime while under the influence of drink, by a fit of murderous mania and a morbid curiosity to observe the process of dying. A moment after the commission of the crime, I experienced the deepest sorrow of it, and would have done anything in the world to undo it."

Conway told the priest that he believed that he would be saved from the gallows if just one good man would pray for his salvation. Father Bronte did not pursue this line of thought and instead offered to give Conway the Last Sacraments of the Catholic Church for the dying, but the condemned man refused, protesting that he was not fit to receive them.

At around this time, some confusion arose when Conway claimed that his real name was actually Owen Giblin, but that he had changed it to John Conway to avoid a court martial after deserting from the army. This claim was deemed irrelevant to the case and certainly did not warrant a stay of execution, and so, on the Thursday morning of 20 August 1891, a trembling John Conway found himself standing on the wooden trap door of the prison gallows, poised between life and death. As hangman Berry was adjusting the white cap over his head, the old man shuddered and cried out in anguish, "Lord have mercy on my soul. Oh my God! Oh my God!"

The thick noose was placed around his neck and adjusted by Berry's hands, and the old man began to urinate. The lever was thrown. Instead of instant oblivion, John Conway plunged to an horrific, gruesome death. His strapped-up body twitched on the floor below the scaffold, and jets of blood squirted from the torn arteries of his neck. Those who witnessed the hanging saw that Conway's head was barely attached to his body by a thin length of glistening red muscle fibres. The outline of his mouth could be faintly seen, opening and closing against the fabric of the white hood for well over a minute. James Berry, in calculating the drop, had overlooked the frailty of the old man, and the weakness of his neck muscles had almost resulted in a complete decapitation.

That should have been the end of the tragedy of Nicholas Martin, but not long after the botched execution, an irate carpenter in Dublin named Owen Giblin read of the John Conway case in the newspapers, and he produced various papers and documents which showed, beyond a shadow of a doubt, that he was the real Owen Giblin. The carpenter was furious at the association of his name with such a heinous child murderer, and claimed that Conway had stolen his identity.

Therefore, the question remains: who on earth was John Conway, alias John Hooper, Alias Owen Giblin, hanged in 1891 for the senseless, brutal murder of an innocent Liverpool child?

Newspaper cutting from the Evening Express

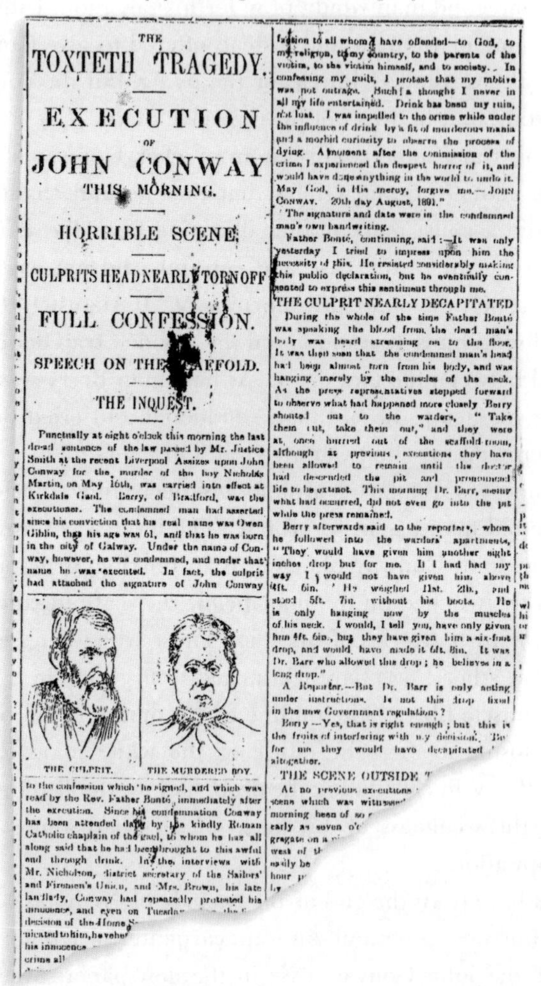

THE

TOXTETH TRAGEDY.

EXECUTION

OF

JOHN CONWAY

THIS MORNING.

HORRIBLE SCENE.

CULPRITS HEAD NEARLY TORN OFF

FULL CONFESSION.

SPEECH ON THE SCAFFOLD.

THE INQUEST.

Punctually at eight o'clock this morning the last dread sentence of the law passed by Mr. Justice Smith at the recent Liverpool Assizes upon John Conway for the murder of the boy Nicholas Martin, on May 16th, was carried into effect at Kirkdale Gaol. Berry, of Bradford, was the executioner. The condemned man had asserted since his conviction that his real name was Owen Giblin, that his age was 61, and that he was born in the city of Galway. Under the name of Conway, however, he was condemned, and under that name he was executed. In fact, the culprit had attached the signature of John Conway

THE CULPRIT.

THE MURDERED BOY.

to the confession which he signed, and which was read by the Rev. Father Bonté, immediately after the execution. Since his condemnation Conway has been attended daily by the kindly Roman Catholic chaplain of the gaol, to whom he has all along said that he had been brought to this awful end through drink. In the interviews with Mr. Nicholson, district secretary of the Sailors' and Firemen's Union, and Mrs. Brown, his late landlady, Conway had repeatedly protested his innocence, and even on Tuesday [illegible] decision of the Home S[illegible] nicated to him, he vehe[illegible] his innocence [illegible] crime all [illegible]

fession to all whom I have offended—to God, to my religion, to my country, to the parents of the victim, to the victim himself, and to society. In confessing my guilt, I protest that my motive was not outrage. Such a thought I never in all my life entertained. Drink has been my ruin, not lust. I was impelled to the crime while under the influence of drink by a fit of murderous mania and a morbid curiosity to observe the process of dying. A moment after the commission of the crime I experienced the deepest horror of it, and would have done anything in the world to undo it. May God, in His mercy, forgive me.—JOHN CONWAY. 20th day August, 1891."

The signature and date were in the condemned man's own handwriting.

Father Bonté, continuing, said:—It was only yesterday I tried to impress upon him the necessity of this. He resisted considerably making this public declaration, but he eventually consented to express this sentiment through me.

THE CULPRIT NEARLY DECAPITATED

During the whole of the time Father Bonté was speaking the blood from the dead man's body was heard streaming on to the floor. It was then seen that the condemned man's head had been almost torn from his body, and was hanging merely by the muscles of the neck. As the press representatives stepped forward to observe what had happened more closely Berry shouted out to the warders, "Take them out, take them out," and they were at once hurried out of the scaffold room, although at previous executions they have been allowed to remain until the doctor had descended the pit and pronounced life to be extinct. This morning Dr. Barr, seeing what had occurred, did not even go into the pit while the press remained.

Berry afterwards said to the reporters, whom he followed into the warders' apartments, "They would have given him another eight inches drop but for me. If I had had my way I would not have given him above 4ft. 6in. He weighed 11st. 2lb., and stood 5ft. 7in. without his boots. He is only hanging now by the muscles of his neck. I would, I tell you, have only given him 4ft. 6in., but they have given him a six-foot drop, and would have made it 6ft. 8in. It was Dr. Barr who allowed this drop; he believes in a long drop."

A Reporter.—But Dr. Barr is only acting under instructions. Is not this drop fixed in the new Government regulations?

Berry.—Yes, that is right enough; but this is the fruits of interfering with my decision. But for me they would have decapitated [illegible] altogether.

THE SCENE OUTSIDE T[illegible]

At no previous executions [illegible] scene which was witnessed [illegible] morning been of so [illegible] early as seven o'c[illegible] gregate on a [illegible] west of th[illegible] easily be [illegible] hour p[illegible] by [illegible]

Seraphim Joe Fortes

Joe Fortes

The secret Daredevil Club met on the first Thursday of every month at their luxurious premises on Liverpool's Duke Street. The club was made up of some sixty members from all walks of life, whose main purpose was to devise and carry out a myriad of perilous dares and madcap challenges.

One August night in 1881, one of the devil-may-care members of the clandestine Duke Street club, challenged any of his fellow members to swim across the River Mersey in the dead of night. If any of them could achieve this risky and formidable feat of endurance, he would be awarded one thousand guineas.

Within days, Captain Wagstaff, an elderly member of the social establishment, made arrangements to introduce a teenager, who went by the name of Seraphim Joe Fortes, into the club. From some there were gasps of revulsion – merely because the youth happened to be black. Seraphim was a swimming instructor at the St George's Baths at the Pier Head, the son of a Barbadian farmer and his Spanish wife, who had come to Liverpool as a child on a British windjammer. With his own eyes, Captain Wagstaff had seen

Seraphim swim the 1,312 yards from the Albert Dock to Woodside, Birkenhead, allegedly to visit a young Irish girl! Captain Wagstaff paid the club membership fee for his protégé – and promptly entered him into a cross-Mersey race between two other members of the Daredevil Club – John McNaughten, and Zalech Goldstein.

At midnight on Wednesday, 31 August 1881, the three contenders dived from the landing stage into the freezing black waters of the River Mersey. Within minutes, McNaughten had succumbed to the biting cold and with numbed limbs, barely managed to swim against the strong current back to the shore. With the help of a policeman he clambered, exhausted, up the slippery, weed-coated steps of the Chester Basin, Mann Island. The policeman who helped to rescue McNaughten agreed not to report the incident after being given a sizeable bribe by Captain Wagstaff.

Within twenty-five minutes, Fortes had easily won the race, and even swam back to the middle of the river to rescue cramp-stricken Goldstein. Goldstein had made elaborate preparations for the race, including imbibing several glasses of brandy and coating his body with a thick layer of grease. Fortes steered him through the strong currents back to the safety of the landing stage, where Wagstaff, the bribed policeman, and a number of members of the Daredevil Club, waited with blankets and rum. The prize money was split between Fortes and Wagstaff, with the captain taking almost seventy per cent of the winnings.

Not long after the cross-river race, Seraphim was entered into an official swimming race, and again the object was to cross the Mersey. The Barbadian teenager accomplished the swim with ease and was presented with a gold medal by the Lord Mayor's young daughter. Weeks after that, buoyed up by his recent success, Seraphim accepted a wager from a street bookmaker who bet him three hundred guineas that he could not swim from the Langton Dock to the New Brighton shore in forty minutes or less. Seraphim Joe swam the distance in just under half an hour and whilst he was in the river he left a burly associate to keep watch on the bookmaker, in case he disappeared with the prize money. Crowds of people gathered at New Brighton to cheer Seraphim on and the oyster stalls set up on the shore did a roaring trade that day.

In 1885, after a lucrative spell of exhibition swimming at Blackpool, Seraphim Joe Fortes left Liverpool on a barque called the Robert Kerr, bound for a new life in Vancouver. As it neared its destination the ship ran aground, and its wreck – with Seraphim onboard – was towed to Vancouver, which was then nothing more than a small developing community known as Gastown. Seraphim set to work as a shoeshine boy, handyman and porter at a hotel, before becoming a barman at the Bodega Saloon.

Then, on 13 June 1886, a massive fire swept through the infant city, destroying everything in its path in just twenty minutes. Seraphim Joe Fortes was one of the people responsible for the rebuilding of Gastown, which he now regarded as home. He fell in love with the wide expanse of Vancouver's English Bay and he pitched a tent so that he could live right there on the beach, where he worked as an unpaid lifeguard and swimming instructor. He voluntarily taught hundreds of children to swim, and was eventually paid for his services to the community. Seraphim was made a constable after saving over one hundred lives in the deceptively calm waters of the cove, and the children of English Bay loved Big Joe Fortes, who was always on hand down on the beach, or on patrol in his little boat, should they get into difficulties. He was a wonderful storyteller and told them fabulous tales of the sea and, of course, he was also an expert swimming instructor, who taught them every style of swimming.

As Vancouver grew, so did Seraphim's reputation, and he managed to change many prejudiced attitudes towards him through his ceaseless duties at English Bay.

In February 1922, at the age of fifty-seven, the much-loved Seraphim died of pneumonia, and the city staged a public funeral, attended by hundreds of Vancouver's citizens. But it was the children who had known the big friendly lifeguard who missed him the most. A memorial drinking fountain was erected in Alexandria Park in 1927 by the people of Vancouver, and the inscription upon that granite monument reads: 'Fortes – Little Children Loved Him'.

Other titles by Tom Slemen

HAUNTED LIVERPOOL 1	Tom Slemen	£5.99
HAUNTED LIVERPOOL 2	Tom Slemen	£5.99
HAUNTED LIVERPOOL 3	Tom Slemen	£5.99
HAUNTED LIVERPOOL 4	Tom Slemen	£5.99
HAUNTED LIVERPOOL 5	Tom Slemen	£5.99
HAUNTED LIVERPOOL 6	Tom Slemen	£5.99
HAUNTED LIVERPOOL 7	Tom Slemen	£5.99
HAUNTED LIVERPOOL 8	Tom Slemen	£5.99
HAUNTED LIVERPOOL 9	Tom Slemen	£5.99
HAUNTED LIVERPOOL 10	Tom Slemen	£5.99
HAUNTED LIVERPOOL 11	Tom Slemen	£5.99
HAUNTED LIVERPOOL 12	Tom Slemen	£5.99
HAUNTED LIVERPOOL 13	Tom Slemen	£5.99
HAUNTED LIVERPOOL ANTHOLOGY	Tom Slemen	£6.99
HAUNTED WIRRAL	Tom Slemen	£5.99
LIVERPOOL GHOST WALK	Tom Slemen	£5.99
HAUNTED CHESHIRE	Tom Slemen	£5.99
WICKED LIVERPOOL	Tom Slemen	£5.99
HAUNTED LIVERPOOL double cassette and audio book read by	Tom Slemen	£8.99

Available from all good bookshops. For a free stocklist contact:

The Bluecoat Press
19 Rodney Street
Liverpool L1 9EF

Telephone: 0151 707 2390
Website: www.bluecoatpress.co.uk

If you have had a paranormal encounter, or a supernatural experience of any sort, please drop a line to Tom Slemen c/o the above address.